i Think: World History

Ancient Greece

by Kendra Corr
and Sharon Coletti

© InspirEd Educators, Inc.   Atlanta, Georgia

** It is the goal of InspirEd Educators to create instructional materials that are interesting, engaging, and challenging. Our student-centered approach incorporates both content and skills, placing particular emphasis on reading, writing, vocabulary development, and critical and creative thinking in the content areas.

Edited by Sharon Coletti and Kendra Corr

Cover graphics by Sharon Coletti and Print1 Direct

Copyright © 2008 by InspirEd Educators, Inc

ISBN # 978-1-933558-43-1

Printed in the United States of America

About InspirEd Educators

InspirEd Educators was founded in 2000 by author Sharon Coletti. Our mission is to provide interesting, student-centered, and thought-provoking instructional materials. To accomplish this, we design lesson plans with research-based content information presented in various ways and used as the vehicle for developing critical and creative thinking, reading, writing, collaboration, problem-solving, and other necessary and enduring skills. By requiring students to THINK, our lessons ensure FAR greater retention than simple memorization of facts!

Initially our company offered large, comprehensive, multi-disciplinary social studies curricula. Then in 2008 we joined forces with another small company and author, Kendra Corr, and launched a second line of thematic units, many excerpted and adapted from our original products. These flexible and affordable resources are ideal for individual, small, or large-group instruction. We hope you will find our company's unique approach valuable and that we can serve you again in the near future.

If you are interested in our other offerings, you can find information on our main website at **www.inspirededucators.com**. Additional products are also available at **www.inspirededhomeschoolers.com**.

InspirEd Educators materials provide engaging lesson plans that vary daily and include:

- Lesson-specific Springboards (warm-ups)
- Writing Activities
- Critical and creative thinking
- Problem-solving
- Test-taking skill development
- Primary source analyses (DBQ's)
- Multiple perspectives
- Graphic analyses
- Fascinating readings
- Simulations
- Story-telling
- Practical use of technology
- Debates
- Plays
- Research
- Graphic organizers
- AND SO MUCH MORE!!!!!

Thank you for choosing our units,
Sharon Coletti, President
InspirEd Educators

Tips for Teaching with InspirEd Educators Units

- Before beginning the unit, take time to look through the Objectives and lessons. This will give you a chance to think about what you want to emphasize and decide upon any modifications, connections, or extensions you'd like to include.

- Give your student(s) the Objective worksheet at the beginning of unit study. The Objectives serve as an outline of the content to be covered and provide a means to review information. Have the student(s) define the vocabulary terms as they progress through the lessons and thoroughly answer the essential questions. You can review their responses as you go along or wait and check everything as a test review. It is important that your student(s) have some opportunity to receive feedback on their Objective answers, since assessments provided at the end of the unit are based on these.

- Read through each lesson's materials before beginning. This will help you better understand lesson concepts; decide when and how to present the vocabulary and prepare the handouts (or transparencies) you will need.

- "Terms to know" can be introduced at the beginning of lessons or reviewed at the end, unless specified otherwise. (In a few instances the intent is for students to discover the meanings of the terms.)

- Look over what we have given you and use whatever you feel your student(s) need. Suggestions are sometimes offered for enrichment, but feel free to use any lesson as a jumping-off point to pursue other topics of interest.

- Our materials are intended to prompt discussion. Often students' answers may vary, but it's important that they be able to substantiate their opinions and ideas with facts. Let the discussion flow!

- Note that differentiated assessments are provided at the end of the unit. Feel free to use any of these as appropriate; cut-and-paste to revise, or create your own tests as desired.

- For additional information and research sites refer to the Resource Section in the back of the unit.

- InspirEd Educators units are all about thinking and creativity, so allow yourself the freedom to adapt the materials as you see fit. Our goal is to provide a springboard for you to jump from in your teaching and your student(s)' learning.

- ENJOY! We at InspirEd Educators truly believe that teaching and learning should be enjoyable, so we do our best to make our lessons interesting and varied. We want you and your student(s) to love learning!

Table θf Contents

Ancient Greece Objectives

Vocabulary - Be able to define and use the following unit terms:

- climate
- terrain
- civilization
- peninsula
- city-state
- mythology
- archaeologist
- deity
- ritual
- clan
- plunder
- culture
- polis
- nobility
- merchant
- reform
- democracy
- citizen
- lottery
- staple
- textiles
- colony
- artisan
- marathon
- legend
- strait
- alliance
- Golden Age
- anthropomorphic
- moral
- Socratic method
- corruption
- philosophy
- political science
- biology
- mortal
- oracle
- pentathlon
- truce
- architecture
- superstition
- ethics
- theorem
- physics
- treasury
- siege
- province
- empire

Fully answer the following questions:
1. Describe the geography and climate of Greece.
2. Explain the characteristics of the earliest inhabitants of ancient Greece.
3. Describe the important elements of the Greek city-state.
4. Describe the characteristics of Greek democracy.
5. Explain how Greek lands and resources affected their economy.
6. Explain the significance of the Persian Wars.
7. Describe the different genres and purposes of Greek literature.
8. Explain the significance of Socrates and his students.
9. Explain mythology and why it was important to the ancient Greeks.
10. Describe the purpose of the ancient Olympics.
11. Describe the scientific contributions of the ancient Greeks.
12. Explain what factors led to the decline and fall of Greek civilization.

Ancient Greece Objectives - Suggestions for Answers

Vocabulary - Be able to define and use the following unit terms:
Terms are defined in the lesson in which they are introduced.

Fully answer the following questions:

1. *Ancient Greece enjoyed mild temperatures, close proximity to water and lots of mountains that provided protection. However, the rugged terrain, lack of farmable land, and mountains were also disadvantageous in terms of travel and communication among the people of the land.*

2. *The Minoans were the first civilization, a lively, happy people who served as a cultural bridge between Europe and the Middle East. The Mycenaeans were more warlike. The Dorians were invaders from the north who created chaos at the beginning of the Dark Ages. They eventually merged with the Greeks who were there before them.*

3. *Although each city-state developed independently from one another, most had similar layouts and elements such as an acropolis (fortified hill), and an agora (marketplace and public meeting place).*

4. *Greek citizenship applied to all men, age 18 and older, who were born in Greece and had completed their military service. Active participation in government affairs was not something they took lightly, as all were supposed to attend and vote in the Assembly. Other offices and leaders were chosen by lottery or were elected by the Assembly.*

5. *Since the Greeks did not have enough land, they established colonies which enabled them to use their time, effort, and land to grow and produce tradable items such as grapes, olives, and wine. This enabled them to become the leading commercial sea power of the ancient world.*

6. *The Greeks gained confidence from beating the formidable Persian Empire. They gained control of the Aegean region, removed the Persian threat in the area, and entered their Golden Age. This was a time in which numerous achievements in literature, science, philosophy and the like were produced. These contributions would influence Europe and beyond for years to come.*

7. *Poems were used to teach Greek values, plays were used to poke fun at government and other issues (comedies), and fables taught morality.*

8. *Socrates was the world's first philosopher (a thinker and seeker of truth and reason) who studied ideas and ethics. He taught his students (Plato and Aristotle) to discover truth by asking questions. The Socratic Method, his way of questioning his students, is still used in education today.*

9. *Mythology was the religion of the Greeks which helped them explain their world and natural phenomena.*

10. *The ancient Greek Olympics were held to honor Zeus. While the competitions were athletic in nature, they were held for religious purposes.*

11. *The Greeks contributed many ideas in science (hydraulics), medicine (scientific, rather than religious), and math (Pythagorean Theorem).*

12. *The Peloponnesian Wars led to depopulation, destruction, loss of leadership, unemployment, and a weakened polis. It was then easy for the Macedonians, under Phillip II to conquer and take over the region. However, Phillip's son Alexander the Great, admired the Greeks so much that he spread their ideas and culture throughout his huge empire, where it was all preserved.*

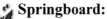

> **Springboard:**
> Students should read "Greece Lightning (and Other Conditions)"
> and answer the questions.

Objective: The student will study the geographical features and characteristics of ancient Greece.

Materials:

Greece Lightning (Springboard handout)
The Aegean World (handout)
The Lay of the Land (handout)

Terms to know:

climate - the weather in a particular place over a long period of time
terrain - the surface of the ground
civilization - a society with a high level of social and political organization, as well as advanced levels of achievement (including writing)
peninsula - land surrounded by water on three sides

Procedure:

- After reviewing the Springboard, explain that _in this lesson, the student(s) will examine the geographical characteristics of Greece and predict whether or not they will help this civilization grow, or hinder its progress_.
- Distribute "The Aegean World" and "The Lay of the Land." The student(s) should work individually, in pairs, or small groups to complete the handout. Remind them that they should also use information from the Springboard to complete the chart.
- Have the student(s) share and compare their answers and discuss.

Greece Lightning (and Other Conditions)

If you were to visit the country of Greece, you would most likely have good weather since the sun shines most of the time, except during the winter months when it is more likely to be cloudy and rainy. Greece, which is located at the southern tip of the Balkan Peninsula, has what is called a "Mediterranean climate." The term describes a special kind of climate with hot, dry summers and mild, moist winters. Since there can be dramatic differences in rainfall from year to year, the natural plant life in Greece consists mainly of drought-tolerant, woody shrubs and trees, and fall grasses. Greek crops include wheat, corn, barley, sugar beets, olives, tomatoes, wine grapes, tobacco, and potatoes.

Mediterranean climates are found mainly along the west (windward) coasts of continents, usually between 30° and 40° north or south latitude, and include the central Chilean coast, the central and southern California coast, the southern tip of Africa, portions of southwestern Australia, and of course the region surrounding the Mediterranean Sea as well as nearby Portugal and Morocco.

Which term does **NOT** describe WEATHER conditions in Greece?
    A. sunny   B. cloudy   C. raining   D. mild

_____ is the _____ over a long period of time.
    A. Climate … weather
    B. Mediterranean … Sea
    C. Greece … plant life
    D. Weather … conditions

Complete the analogy:
    Hot and dry is to summers, as _____.

Woody shrubs, trees, and fall grasses
    A. require frequent rainfall.
    B. are among Greece's crops.
    C. can live through droughts.
    D. need variations in rainfall.

All of these places have a Mediterranean climate, **EXCEPT**
    A. the coast of Chile.
    B. eastern California.
    C. southern Australia.
    D. Italy and Spain.

If you were to visit the country of Greece, you would most likely have good weather, since the sun shines most of the time, except during the winter months when it is more likely to be cloudy and rainy. Greece, which is located at the southern tip of the Balkan Peninsula, has what is called a "Mediterranean climate." The term describes a special kind of climate with hot, dry summers and mild, moist winters. Since there can be dramatic differences in rainfall from year to year, the natural plant life in Greece consists mainly of drought-tolerant, woody shrubs and trees, and fall grasses. Greek crops include wheat, corn, barley, sugar beets, olives, tomatoes, wine grapes, tobacco, and potatoes.

Mediterranean climates are found mainly along the west (windward) coasts of continents, usually between 30° and 40° north or south latitude, and include the central Chilean coast, the central and southern California coast, the southern tip of Africa, portions of southwestern Australia, and of course the region surrounding the Mediterranean Sea as well as nearby Portugal and Morocco.

Which term does **NOT** describe WEATHER conditions in Greece?
  A. sunny   B. cloudy   C. raining   D. mild *
(A-C all describe a condition on a particular day or weather. Mild describes the overall weather conditions or climate.)

_____ is the _____ over a long period of time.
  A. Climate … weather *
  B. Mediterranean … Sea
  C. Greece … plant life
  D. Weather … conditions

(Climate is defined as the weather conditions in a place over a long period of time.)

Complete the analogy:
Hot and dry is to summers, as _____ **mild and moist is to winters.** _____ .
  (While this was a pretty simple analogy, the trick is to make up a sentence that is true for both parts of the analogy. For example, "Hot and dry describes Greece's climate in the summer, as mild and moist describe Greece's climate in the winter.)

Woody shrubs, trees, and fall grasses
  A. require frequent rainfall.
  B. are among Greece's crops.
  C. can live through droughts. *
  D. need variations in rainfall.

(The term "drought-resistant" means that the plants can survive droughts. These plants are not crops, since they grow naturally.)

All of these places have a Mediterranean climate, **EXCEPT**
  A. the coast of Chile.
  B. eastern California. *
  C. southern Australia.
  D. Italy and Spain.
(Though not exactly as in the passage, A and C are mentioned and students should know Italy and Spain are on the Mediterranean. Also California has no east coast.)

THE AEGEAN WORLD

BLACK SEA

AEGEAN SEA

ASIA MINOR

GREECE

IONIAN SEA

MEDITERRANEAN
SEA

50   100 miles

50   100 150 200 250 kilometers

CRETE

NOTES

- GREECE ITSELF IS FAIRLY SMALL.
- GREY SHADED AREAS ARE MOUNTAINS AND OTHER RUGGED TERRAINS.
- MOUNTAIN VALLEYS HAVE VERY FERTILE SOIL
- THERE ARE NO MAJOR RIVERS
- CIVILIZATIONS DEVELOPED ON CRETE AND OTHER ISLANDS, MAINLAND GREECE AND THE COAST OF THE ASIA MINOR.

The Lay of the Land

DIRECTIONS: Use information from "Greece Lightning (and Other Conditions)" and "The Aegean World" map. List the seven geographic features and predict what you think the impact of each would be on the development of ancient Greece.

Characteristic	Impact	Positive or Negative?

Characteristic	Impact	Positive or Negative?
Mild temperatures: hot in summer, cold in the winter	*The Greeks enjoyed a pleasant climate without extremes in temperatures. Their crops would grow well and enable them to thrive.*	*Positive.*
Unpredictable rainfall	*Have to grow crops that do not require a lot of water such as wheat, barley, olives, or wine grapes. This will affect what they produce and trade.*	*Somewhat negative because they are limited in what they can grow.*
Peninsula and islands urrounded by water (Mediterranean Sea, Ionian Sea, Aegean Sea, Black Sea)	*Everyone is close to water. Easy access to the water makes it easy to travel and trade with others. They also can live off the water by fishing. The people living on islands have a fixed amount of land they can live on.*	*Both: Positive because they have a way of traveling and trading and access to food. Negative because it limits the amount of land they have.*
No major rivers or other inland water sources	*Once away from the coast, travel is difficult. Also, the lack of rivers, lakes, etc makes it hard to get water to their crops if rainfall is low.*	*Negative.*
Most of the land is rugged, rough, or mountainous.	*Makes travel over land very difficult. Makes communications between settlements very difficult. Provides protection because the settlements are difficult to get to.*	*Both: Negative because it's hard to get around by land so people could not easily communicate. Positive because of the protection that mountains provide.*
Lots of mountain valleys which have fertile soil.	*Crops will thrive in fertile soil. They can grow more food and other goods to feed everyone and trade the surplus. This will help people live better and get rich.*	*Positive.*
Settlement areas are very spread out and separated by water (islands) and/or rough, mountainous terrain.	*The various settlements will not have a lot of contact with each other. They will develop their own identities and be independent of each other.*	*Both: Positive because people will have a strong sense of their own communities but negative if it creates divisions.*

The Family Tree

Springboard:
Students should study the "____" timeline and answer the questions.

Objective: The student will be able to identify and describe the early peoples of ancient Greece.

Materials:
"_____" (Springboard handout)
The Relatives (3 handouts)
Who's Who? (3 handouts)
highlighters (optional)

Terms to know:
city-state - an independent, self-governing city and the territory around it
mythology - stories of gods, goddesses, and heroes
archaeologist - one who studies remains of the past
deity - a god or goddess
ritual - religious ceremony
clan - group of families related by common ancestors
plunder - rob and damage
culture - way of life, shared values, and behavior of a group of people

Procedure:
- After reviewing the Springboard, explain that *in this lesson the student(s) will learn about the three groups of people who settled the area which became Ancient Greece: the Mycenaeans, the Minoans, and the Dorians.*
- Distribute the three "The Relatives" handouts. The student(s) should work individually, in pairs, or small groups to read the three handouts, underlining or highlighting important information or passages.
- Then distribute the "Who's Who?" handouts. The student(s) should use the graphic organizers to organize their thoughts and identify the most important points about each group. They should then create acrostic poems, describing each group with words or phrases that begin with each letter of their names. Explain to the student(s) that *the words and phrases should specifically describe points about the each of the groups*.
- Have the student(s) share and compare their poems and discuss.

- **EXTENSION:** Have the student(s) pick one of the groups and do further online or other media research about their culture and everyday life. The research could then be presented in a poster or essay.

"_____"

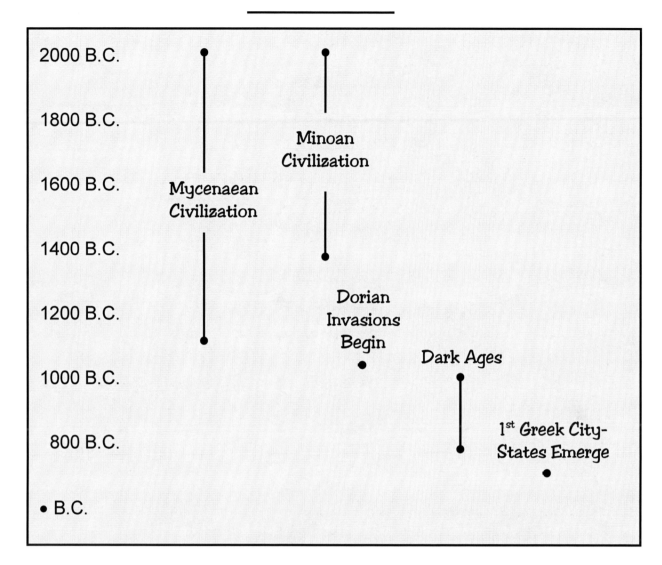

2000 B.C.	
1800 B.C.	Minoan Civilization
1600 B.C.	Mycenaean Civilization
1400 B.C.	
1200 B.C.	Dorian Invasions Begin
1000 B.C.	Dark Ages
800 B.C.	1st Greek City-States Emerge
• B.C.	

Which of these statements is **NOT** supported by the timeline?
  A. The Mycenaean civilization lasted longer than the Minoan civilization.
  B. The Dorian invasions began a short time before the Dark Ages started.
  C. The Dorians ruled Greece through the period known as the Dark Ages.
  D. The first city-states did not appear in Greece until after the Dark Ages.

Which of these statements is **NOT** a logical prediction based on the timeline?
  A. The Dorian invasions had a lot to do with the downfall of the Minoans.
  B. The chaos of the Dorian invasions likely led to the Dark Ages of Greece.
  C. A period of growth and stability followed a period of decline and chaos.
  D. There were at least three main groups of early peoples in ancient Greece.

A good title for this timeline would be
  A. "Wars of Ancient Greece."
  B. "Who's Who in Ancient Greece?"
  C. "The Beginning of Greek Civilization"
  D. "Good Times and Bad Times of Greece."

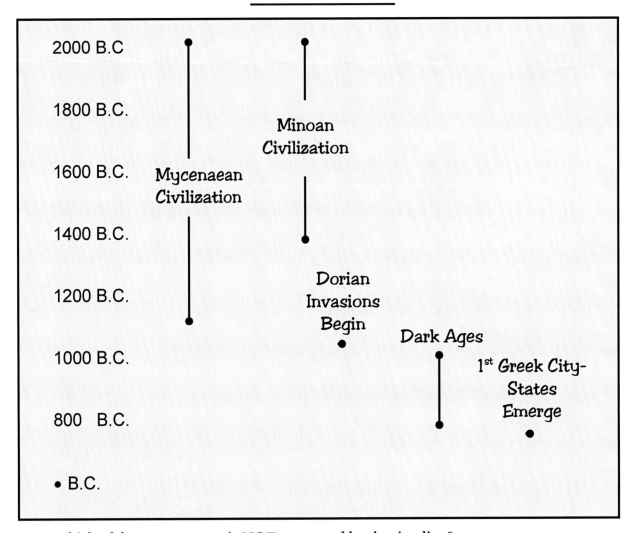

Which of these statements is **NOT** supported by the timeline?
   A. The Mycenaean civilization lasted longer than the Minoan civilization.
   B. The Dorian invasions began a short time before the Dark Ages started.
   C. The Dorians ruled Greece through the period known as the Dark Ages. *
   D. The first city–states did not appear in Greece until after the Dark Ages.
   (Choices A, B, and D are all true based on the dates on the timeline.)

Which of these statements is **NOT** a logical prediction based on the timeline?
   A. The Dorian invasions had a lot to do with the downfall of the Minoans. *
   B. The chaos of the Dorian invasions likely led to the Dark Ages of Greece.
   C. A period of growth and stability followed a period of decline and chaos.
   D. There were at least three main groups of early peoples in ancient Greece.
   (A is not logical because the end of the Minoan civilization came at least 300 years before the Dorian invasions. All others make sense based on timeline information.)

A good title for this timeline would be
   A. "Wars of Ancient Greece."
   B. "Who's Who in Ancient Greece?"
   C. "The Beginning of Greek Civilization" *
   D. "Good Times and Bad Times of Greece."

(Choices A, B, and D are too broad for the events on the timeline. Choice C correctly summarizes the content of the timeline.)

The Relatives: The Minoans

The first advanced civilization of what would become Ancient Greece developed on the island of Crete by about 2000 B.C. The Minoans, named for King Minos, a ruler from Greek mythology, were influenced by other civilizations around the Mediterranean Sea such as the Egyptians. Much of what is now known about these people is based on the findings of Sir Arthur Evans, an archeologist who in 1898 discovered the remains of the Minoan palace in Knossos. The main rooms of the palace were decorated with frescoes showing scenes from daily life of this early civilization.

Based on the frescoes, we know that the Minoans were a lively and active people who enjoyed life. They were fond of animals, dancing, and sports. One of the most interesting past-times of young Minoans was "bull-leaping," an event in which boys and girls would grab a bull by the horns and flip over its back (at right). The Minoans also built beautiful gardens and were quite skilled at jewelry making.

Like other early Greek civilizations, the Minoans built temples to their gods and goddesses. Their most important deity was the earth mother, or goddess of fertility. Minoans performed many rituals to their gods in temples, but also in private homes, in caves, and on mountaintops.

Due to their location, Minoans made their living by trading their many goods by ship across the Mediterranean and Black Seas. Products they traded included honey, olive oil, wine, gold, and grains. Unlike most early civilizations that relied mainly on farming, the Minoans made their living from the sea.

Their trade brought the Minoans in frequent contact with lands in the Middle East. Later the Greeks would adopt the Minoan's system of writing, gold work, and architecture, ideas which had come to the Minoans from their trading partners in the Middle East.

How the Minoan civilization came to an end is somewhat of a mystery. The height of their civilization was around 1600 B.C. and its collapse was only about 200 years later. Some historians believe that the busy Minoan cities may have been destroyed by volcanoes or perhaps by huge tidal waves that may have crashed to shore following underwater earthquakes. Although the exact cause of its collapse is unknown, the Minoan civilization ended in about 1400 B.C. After that time control of the Aegean World shifted to their mainland neighbors, the Mycenaeans.

The Relatives: The Mycenaeans

The Mycenaeans are considered by many scholars to be the first "true" Greeks. This group of people who moved into Europe from Central Asia and eventually made their way south to the Balkan peninsula, where they settled in southern Greece. The Mycenaeans name comes from their most important city, Mycenae. Much of what we know about them comes from the 1870 findings of treasure hunter and archeologist Heinrich Schliemann, who found the city.

Unlike the peace-loving, lively, and happy-go-lucky Minoans, the Mycenaeans were a warlike people. They build their cities with armed fortresses on hillsides, all connected together by huge stone walls. Their art mostly is of battle scenes, and particularly the Trojan War.

Around 1250 B.C. the Mycenaeans launched an attack against Troy, a city in the Asia Minor to the east. Scholars are not sure why they attacked Troy, but it is likely that the city's location (between the Aegean and Black Seas) made it a target. The Mycenaeans spent ten years attacking Troy until, according to the famous story, they presented the Trojans with a giant, wooden statue of a horse and snuck into the city in its belly. As the story goes, the Myceneaens jumped from the horse when they were inside the city gates and slaughtered the Trojans in the middle of the night (picture at right).

For the next half-century or so, tales of the Trojan War would be told and passed from generation to generation. Finally around 750 B.C., a blind poet named Homer included this tale into his famous epics, the *Iliad* and the *Odyssey*.

It is thought that for a time the warlike Mycenaeans fought against each other. Then, once they began to prosper by shipbuilding and sea travel, they joined to form a loose union of kingdoms. While the Mycenaean kingdoms traded with the Minoans and exchanged goods and ideas, the warriors mainly used their newfound sea power to raid and rob their neighbors.

By about 1400 B.C. the Mycenaeans took the place of the Minoans as the most powerful civilization in the region. They held their position of power until around 1200 B.C., and their decline, also, is also a bit of a mystery. Historians usually cite one of two ways to explain their collapse. One is that a natural disaster, such as a drought, caused widespread famine. The other, which seems more reasonable given their warlike ways, is that internal fighting among the kingdoms led to divisions which eventually brought the civilization down. Regardless of the conditions that led their decline, the weakened Mycenaeans were easy prey for a new band of invaders. The Dorians moved into the region from the north around 1100 B.C., bringing an end to the Mycenaean civilization.

The Relatives: The Dorians

There are many theories about the origins of the Dorians. According to Greek mythology, the Dorians' name comes from a city in central Greece called Doris. Stories tell of how a Mycenaean ruler named Eurystheus, drove the three sons of Hercules from Doris and later took revenge by invading the mainland of Greece to reclaim what they saw as their rightful territory. Unlike the Minoans and Mycenaeans, there is little other archeological evidence to offer any other information about these people.

What is known is that the Dorians invaded mainland Greece around 1100 B.C. Although they were not as advanced as the Mycenaeans in most ways, they did have one very important advantage. The iron slashing sword (at left) was much stronger than the bronze swords used by the Mycenaeans. Not only were the Dorians weapons superior, but their warriors arrived in the area at a time when the Mycenaean civilization was already in decline, making them an easy target. The Dorian invasion led to a period of violence and lawlessness known as the Dark Ages. Although few, if any, written records have been found from this period, it is believed that most farm crops were destroyed and trade came to a halt.

Not all was lost, however. Those Mycenaeans who were able to flee the Dorian invasion, either went to the Aegean islands or to the western coast of the Asia Minor (later known as Ionia), where their Greek traditions were preserved. Those Mycenaeans left on the mainland, mixed with the Dorians to form a new culture.

The new civilization that formed during the chaos following the Dorian invasion was a tribal society. People were organized into clans and ruled by kings. Wealth was based on land ownership, which resulted in a small, rich, and privileged class that controlled the masses. Many people made their living by plundering their neighbors. Finally, the rich landowners grew tired of answering to the greedy kings, who were overthrown by about 750 B.C.

In some areas the Dorians were heavily influenced by the Greek people and adopted many of their ways. The Dorians merged with the mainland Greeks who had not fled during the Dark Ages.

In other areas the Dorians were able to hold onto their power. Such settlements were very warlike and kept to themselves. Eventually, these small, remote villages grew into independent communities known as city-states. These small, independently ruled cities grew and thrived and eventually developed many of the ideas, knowledge and culture that are known in history as belonging to Ancient Greece.

Who's Who?

Origins:

Important Dates/Events:

Descriptive Words:

What Happened to Them?

MINOANS

_____

_____

_____

_____

_____

_____

_____

_____

Who's Who?

Origins: Important Dates/Events:

Descriptive Words: What Happened to Them?

MYCENAEANS

_____

_____

_____

_____

_____

_____

_____

_____

_____

Who's Who?

Origins:

Important Dates/Events:

Descriptive Words:

What Happened to Them?

DORIANS

_____

_____

_____

_____

_____

_____

_____

_____

Polis! Polis!

Objective: The student will be able to describe the diversity among the cultures of the various Greek city-states.

Materials: The Greek City-State (Springboard handout)
Profiling a Polis (handout)
Our Town (handout)

Terms to know: **polis** - city

Procedure:

• While reviewing the Springboard, point out that *while all city-states had a similar layout and elements, each developed independently from the others, so all of the city-states had their own distinctive personalities and cultures.*

• Distribute "Profiling a Polis" and one or more (see instructions below) "Our Town" handouts.

 • **For full class instruction** have students work in small groups to research one of the following city-states: **Argos, Athens, Corinth, Megara,** or **Sparta.** They should use the Internet, textbooks, and other media sources to find information to complete the note-taking guide and then complete the "Our Town" handout for their city-state.

• **For individualized instruction** have the student research at least two of the city-states listed above, completing "Profiling a Polis" note taking form for each. Then, he/she should complete "Our Town" for one or all of the city-states researched.

• Have the student(s) present their handouts and information, highlighting what they found to be unique about each city-state. *(Basic information:*
Argos - *Located inland in central part of the peninsula on a fertile plain; nearby port allowed trade; often credited with inventing coinage; governed as a monarchy; advanced in art, sculpture, and drama.*
Athens - *On eastern part of the peninsula; people greatly valued education (for males), art, literature, and philosophy; Athena was their patron goddess; became leader of city-states.*
Corinth - *A port in the center of the peninsula; was a major trading center; ruled by a king and his advisors; education, art, etc. important, though not as advanced as Athens; developed coins for trade.*
Megara - *Also a port city; great sailors, explorers, and traders; learned about and developed coinage; considered themselves educational rivals to Athens (who would have disagreed); famous for textiles; founded city of Byzantium (later Constantinople and then Istanbul, Turkey); Sparta's ally in Peloponnesian War.*
Sparta - *At southern tip of Greek peninsula; valued military and physical strength; males removed from homes and trained from age 7; ruled by small group of generals.*

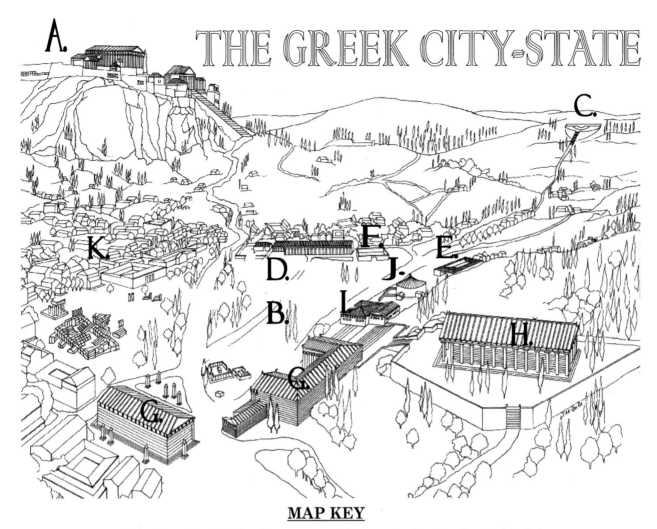

THE GREEK CITY-STATE

MAP KEY

A. The Acropolis - Fortified hill where a temple was built for the local deity

B. The Agora - Open meeting place and where people go to market

C. The Assembly - Place citizens met to discuss and vote on laws and other matters

D. The Fountainhouse - Place where women came to draw water and socialize

E. The Strategeion - Where military leaders met to conduct their business

F. Jail and Law Courts - Building where criminals were housed and trials were held

G. Stoa - Covered walkways usually used by merchants to sell their goods

H. Temple - Building to serve as homes for gods and goddesses

I. The Bouletuerion - Building in which city officials met to conduct their business.

J. The Tholos - Tomb

K. Dwellings -People's homes; dwellings usually surrounded the city.

1. **Which buildings or places do you think were most important to the daily lives of people in Ancient Greece? Explain.**

2. **Which building or places do you think had the greatest impact on the lives of the people of Ancient Greece? Explain.**

PROFILING  A POLIS

Location/Geography

Government

Economy/Trade

Major / Important Events

City-State

Cultural/Daily Life

Anything Else?

OUR TOWN

DIRECTIONS: DESIGN A FLAG, WRITE A MOTTO, AND DRAW A MASCOT FOR THE CITY-STATE YOU RESEARCHED. THESE ARE TO BE PUT ON DISPLAY AT THE AGORA SO ALL VISITORS WILL KNOW EXACTLY WHAT YOUR TOWN IS ALL ABOUT!

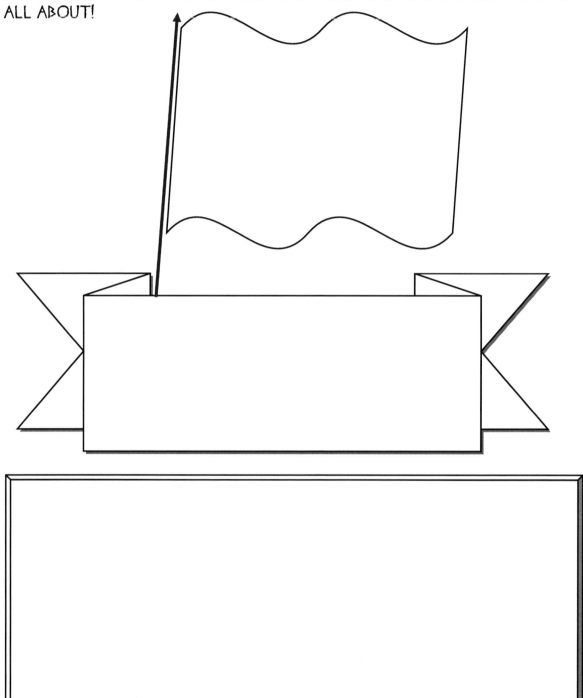

Springboard:
    Students should read "The Birth of Democracy" and answer the questions.

Objective: The student will study the development of democracy in Greece and compare it to American democracy.

Materials:	The Birth of Democracy (Springboard handout) Democracy in Athens (handout) Side by Side (handout)
Terms to know:	**nobility** - upper class, based on birth **merchant** - one who buys, sells, or trades for a living **reform** - change to correct problems in society **democracy** - government by the people **citizen** - active member of a nation or state **lottery** - selection by random drawing

Procedure:
- After reviewing the Springboard, explain that *in this lesson the student(s) will examine the characteristics of democracy in Greece*.
- Distribute "Democracy in Athens" and "Side by Side." Have the student(s) study the chart to become familiar with how the democracy in Athens worked. Depending on prior knowledge and ability level, you can complete the American Democracy section together or have the student(s) complete the entire chart independently. If guided, have the student(s) complete the remainder of the chart individually, in pairs, or small groups.
- The student(s) should then complete the bottom of the handout to compare and contrast the two democracies using the Venn diagram.
- Have the student(s) share and compare their answers and discuss.

The Birth of Democracy

As Greece emerged from its Dark Ages, it was a tribal society organized into clans and ruled by kings. Most city-states grew tired of the kings, though, and by the 700's B.C., the nobility took over and formed small councils that made all the decisions. The *oligarchies* eventually weakened due to tensions between the nobles and common people.

Merchants, in particular challenged the power of the ruling class. They had grown very rich from trade and were no longer willing to accept privilege and land ownership based on birth. The lower classes also had their complaints. Since they had no land of their own, it was difficult for them to support themselves. Often they were forced to borrow from the landowners. In many cases the only way to pay off their debts was to enter into slave-like agreements. In general most Greeks were unhappy with the nobles' rule.

In many city-states military leaders, called tyrants, seized power from the nobles. These military men knew that tension could lead to chaos, and they wanted to end the unrest, bring about reforms, and better the lives of their people. Although some may have been ruthless leaders as the word suggests, many were reformers, called tyrants because they took power by force. Eventually, many city-states began to experiment with a new form of rule. Democracy, a word meaning rule by the "demos" or people, was first established in the city-state of Athens.

During the rule of several "tyrants," Athens' citizens' freedom increased. For example, Cleisthenes, who came to power in Greece in 508 B.C., introduced laws giving people important rights: freedom of speech, the right to assemble, and equality before the law. Over time citizenship expanded to those who did not own land and used a lottery to decide who held offices in government. Although democracy in Athens was the first, it was not the most inclusive. Citizenship did not apply to women, slaves, or anyone who was not born in the city-state. Other Greek city-states also went from monarchies to oligarchies to democracies, some giving rights to a wider range of people.

Based on information from the passage, an "oligarchy" is the rule by
- A. one strong leader.
- B. hereditary kings.
- C. citizens or people.
- D. a privileged few.

According to the passage, the tyrants were not necessarily
- A. ruthless.
- B. military.
- C. Greek.
- D. kings.

Cleistenes would **BEST** be described as
- A. the first leader of a democratic government.
- B. the first elected leader of a Greek democracy.
- C. a tyrant who helped establish democracy in Athens.
- D. a ruthless ruler who gained and held power by force.

The passage supports that idea that democracy can only emerge if there is
- A. women, slaves, and foreigners are allowed citizenship.
- B. no power is given to those with land, wealth, and privilege.
- C. a concern for the value and worth of individual citizens.
- D. an earlier form of government that people find unacceptable.

As Greece emerged from its Dark Ages, it was a tribal society organized into clans and ruled by kings. Most city-states grew tired of the kings, though, and by the 700's B.C., the nobility took over and formed small councils that made all the decisions. The *oligarchies* eventually weakened due to tensions between the nobles and common people.

Merchants, in particular challenged the power of the ruling class. They had grown very rich from trade and were no longer willing to accept privilege and land ownership based on birth. The lower classes also had their complaints. Since they had no land of their own, it was difficult for them to support themselves. Often they were forced to borrow from the landowners. In many cases the only way to pay off their debts was to enter into slave-like agreements. In general most Greeks were unhappy with the nobles' rule.

In many city-states military leaders, called tyrants, seized power from the nobles. These military men knew that tension could lead to chaos, and they wanted to end the unrest, bring about reforms, and better the lives of their people. Although some may have been ruthless leaders as the word suggests, many were reformers, called tyrants because they took power by force. Eventually, many city-states began to experiment with a new form of rule. Democracy, a word meaning rule by the "demos" or people, was first established in the city-state of Athens.

During the rule of several "tyrants," Athens' citizens' freedom increased. For example, Cleisthenes, who came to power in Greece in 508 B.C., introduced laws giving people important rights: freedom of speech, the right to assemble, and equality before the law. Over time citizenship expanded to those who did not own land and used a lottery to decide who held offices in government. Although democracy in Athens was the first, it was not the most inclusive. Citizenship did not apply to women, slaves, or anyone who was not born in the city-state. Other Greek city-states also went from monarchies to oligarchies to democracies, some giving rights to a wider range of people.

Based on information from the passage, an oligarchy is the rule of
A. one strong leader.   C. citizens or people.
B. hereditary kings.   D. a privileged few. *
(The term is described in the previous sentence.)

According to the passage, the tyrants were not necessarily
A. ruthless. *   B. military.   C. Greek.   D. kings.
(The tyrants are described as reformers, concerned with the well-being of the people.)

Cleistenes would **BEST** be described as   *(The last paragraph*
A. the first leader of a democratic government.   *explains that some*
B. the first elected leader of a Greek democracy.   *tyrants, including*
C. a tyrant who helped establish democracy in Athens. *   *Cleistenes, increased*
D. a ruthless ruler who gained and held power by force.   *citizens' freedom.)*

The passage supports that idea that democracy can only emerge if there is
A. women, slaves, and foreigners are allowed citizenship.
B. no power is given to those with land, wealth, and privilege.
C. a concern for the value and worth of individual citizens. *
D. an earlier form of government that people find unacceptable.
(A and B are false, and D is only true in some situations.)

DEMOCRACY IN ATHENS

THE ASSEMBLY

- The Assembly was made up of all citizens of Athens (at least 18 years old, male, completed military service).
- The Assembly had four main duties: issue decrees (official orders, such as going to war), elect officials, make the laws, and preside over the courts.
- The Assembly needed at least 6,000 citizens to hold a vote.
- All members could vote on all laws and other decisions.

COUNCIL OF 500

- Set the agenda for the Assembly
- Carried out and oversaw the actions of the Assembly
- 500 members were chosen by lottery for 1 year terms
- No one could serve more than 2 times in their life.
- Terms could not be successive.
- Had to be at least 30 years of age to be on the Council.

ADMINISTRATION

- The most prestigious positions were elected by the Assembly (Board of Ten Generals, City Architect, Priests and Sacred Treasurers).
- Elected positions were not compulsory, but those who wanted them had to nominate themselves.
- Numerous other board positions were chosen by lottery.

COURTS

- 6000 potential jurors were selected by lottery every year from citizens over 30 years of age.
- Each individual case could be heard by a jury of anywhere from 200-2000 members.
- Trials lasted no longer than 1 day.
- Verdicts were decided right away with no time to deliberate or argue.

Side by Side

Greece   **The U.S.**

	Greece	The U.S.
Who participates?		
Who holds power?		
How does one participate?		
How is power distributed?		
How are decisions made?		
How is government organized?		
How are leaders chosen?		

Greece   **BOTH**   **The U.S.**

Side by Side Suggestions for Answers

	Greece	The U.S.
Who participates?	*Citizens were men, over 18, who had completed military service; no women, slaves, or foreigners.*	*All citizens of the United States (everyone born in the U.S. or granted citizenship by the government) participate.*
Who holds power?	*Only those defined as citizens could have power, hold office, or vote; women, slaves, and foreigners were excluded.*	*Elected officials hold power, but are accountable to the citizens through elections.*
How does one participate?	*Citizens could participate by issuing decrees, electing officials, making laws, and presiding over courts.*	*People participate by voting, voicing opinions, running for office, supporting campaigns, writing letters, contributions, etc.*
How is power distributed?	*All citizens were members of the Assembly; others were also in the Council of 500, Administration, or Courts.*	*Power is distributed among three federal branches and also to the states and local governments.*
How are decisions made?	*Decisions were made by direct voting on matters. Some decisions were made by elected officials (such as the Ten Generals).*	*Most decisions are made by high office holders (the president or Congress), who are elected by the people.*
How is government organized?	*The main body was the Assembly; there were three other bodies – the Council, Administration and Courts.*	*Government is organized on the federal, state, and local levels.*
How are leaders chosen?	*Leaders were chosen mostly by lottery. Some positions were held after election by the Assembly.*	*Leaders are chosen by citizen vote.*

Greece	BOTH	The U.S.
• *Citizenship limited to men over 18, who had finished military service* • *All citizens participated in Assembly* • *Some leaders chosen by lottery* • *Citizens voted on all matters* • *Only one level of government* • *Foreigners not allowed to become citizens*	• *Use the concept of "citizen" as someone with the right to participate in government* • *Organized into various branches or bodies* • *Voting is means of participation*	• *Citizenship applies to all people (regardless of age, gender, etc) born in the U.S. – or naturalized* • *Citizens represented by elected officials who govern for them* • *Power shared between federal, state and local governments* • *Leaders chosen by vote of citizens, not lottery*

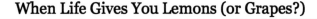

When Life Gives You Lemons (or Grapes?)

Springboard:
Students should complete "Haves and Have Nots."
(1. Answers will vary; 2. Answers will vary but should reference trade as a way to get what is needed; 3. There was limited land available.)

Objective: The student will be able to describe the economic development of the ancient Greeks.

Materials:	Haves and Have Nots (Springboard handout)
	Economic Card Sort (1 cut-out set per student or pair)
	What Ifs... (handout)

Terms to know:

staple - foods that make up a basic diet
textiles - cloth, fabric, or other woven material
colony - settlement ruled by another country
artisan - a skilled craftsperson

Procedure:

- After reviewing the Springboard, explain that *in this lesson the student(s) will further examine the economic situation in Ancient Greece.*

- Distribute the "Economic Card Sort" cards page. The student(s) should work independently or in pairs to cut out the cards, if they aren't already, and then sort them into a logical order.

- Have the student(s) share their order and logic and discuss. *(The correct order is: limited farmland; population grew; established colonies; colonies farmed; Greeks moved to cities; artisans; banking began; trade expanded; new ideas; Greece rich and advanced.)*

- Distribute the "What Ifs..." handout and have the student(s) complete the analysis.

- Have the student(s) share their scenarios and discuss. *(Answers may vary but should be well supported and make sense.)*

Haves and Have Nots

What the Ancient Greeks HAD	What the Ancient Greeks LACKED
• grapes (and good climate and soil to grow them) • olives (and good climate and soil to grow them) • sheep (wool, meat, cheese, milk) • goats (meat, cheese, milk) • islands close by and numerous water routes for travel • metals/mining (iron and bronze)	• a large amount of farmland suitable to grow staple crops such as wheat and other grains • livestock that could feed a large number of people (cows, pigs, etc) • a wide variety of fruits and vegetables • lighter textiles suitable for warm climates (such as cotton)

What do you think the Greeks had that was most important to the success of their economy? Why? _____

_____

_____

_____

What do you think the Greeks lacked that was the greatest obstacle to the success of their economy? How could they overcome the obstacle? _____

_____

_____

_____

Why do you think landowners were so wealthy and powerful in the Ancient Greek civilization? _____

_____

_____

_____

_____

Economic Card Sort

The city-states set up colonies around the Mediterranean coast to grow food to be sent back to Greece.	Instead of farming, people became artisans and made pottery, textiles, and other goods to sell and trade.
Larger ships and harbors were built to keep up with the expanding trade wit other civilizations around the Mediterranean Sea.	As the population of the city-states grew, people could not grow enough food to feed everyone.
Ancient Greece had a very limited amount of usable farmland.	Greece became of the richest, most culturally advanced, and most powerful civilization in the ancient world.
Fewer farmers were needed in Greece so people began to move to growing cities.	The increase in trade led to the exchange of new ideas and goods from different cultures.
Wealthy people began to develop a banking industry by lending money to merchants who wanted to expand their trading businesses.	Colonies grew food staples, so the farmland in Greece could be used to grow crops for trade such as grapes (from which they made wine) and olives.

What Ifs...

DIRECTIONS: For each number, explain how you think the economy of Greece and even Greek history might have been different in each situation described.

WHAT IF there were <u>NO</u> lands available where Greece could establish colonies? _____

_____

_____

_____

_____

_____

WHAT IF Greece's soil was not suitable for growing either staple crops <u>or</u> grapes and olives? _____

_____

_____

_____

_____

_____

WHAT IF the Greeks had <u>NO</u> access to the Sea? _____

_____

_____

_____

_____

_____

WHAT IF the Greeks had <u>enormous</u> amounts of farmable land? ____

_____

_____

_____

_____

_____

_____

_____

Power Struggle

Springboard:
  Students should read "Marathon Man" and answer the questions.

Objective: The student will be able to explain the causes and outcomes of the Persian Wars.

Materials:
  Marathon Man (Springboard handout)
  I, Pericles (2-page handout)
  Making a Long Story Short (handout)
  highlighters (optional)

Terms to know:
  marathon - 26-mile footrace
  legend - story based on fact with fictional details
  strait - narrow body of water that joins together two larger bodies of water
  alliance - group of nations working together for a purpose, such as war
  Golden Age - time of peace and great achievements

Procedure:
- While reviewing the Springboard, explain that _the legend of Pheidippides is part of a larger event in Greek history, the Persian Wars._
- Distribute 'I, Pericles" and have the student(s) read the material, highlighting important or relevant passages.
- Distribute "Making a Long Story Short" and explain that _this format given, participants, causes, events, outcomes, provides a good formula to use when organizing what may seem to be a lot of information._
- Have the student(s) complete the guiding note-taking form independently or in pairs.
- Review the student(s) answers, having them correction and/or add information where appropriate.
- Discuss and have the student(s) respond to the following questions:
  ? Which of the three outcomes do you think is the most beneficial to the Greeks? Why? (_Answers will vary._)
  ? Given the outcomes of the Persian Wars, what do you think is likely to happen to Greece after the war, and why? (_Answers will vary, but will likely include predictions that Greece will prosper and become even more powerful. However their wealth and power could spark further jealousy among Athens' neighbors!_)

marathon man

When the Persian army landed in the Greek city-state of Marathon in 490 B.C., the Athenian army was outnumbered two to one. They sent a foot messenger named Pheidippides to Sparta to get help. It is said that the runner covered the distance of about 140 miles roundtrip in only two days.

Meanwhile the battle at Marathon raged and though outnumbered, the Athenians defeated the mighty Persian army. As the story goes, the Athenians lost just 192 men, while the Persians 6.400 were killed! Eager to send word of the victory back to Athens, Pheidippides was called upon again, this time to run the 26 miles home. When he reached the city steps, he called out, "We are victorious!" and then he collapsed and died on the spot.

Much of what we know about Pheidippides and Ancient Greece comes from the Greek historian, Herodotus, though many question his accounts. In this case why wasn't another messenger sent since Pheidippides had just returned from a 140-mile run? Why didn't he ride a horse? Why would the messenger have died when he was a trained runner? These questions and more have cast some doubt about the tale of the marathon man.

Regardless, this story inspired the modern-day marathon. The event was first run in the 1896 Summer Olympics held in (where else?) Athens, Greece, and was won by a Greek athlete. Though he was slowed down by a crowd that mobbed him at the end of the route, he was the only Greek winner in any track and field event at the 1896 games.

The story of Pheidippides would **BEST** be described as
- A. history.
- B. a legend.
- C. an inspirational tale.
- D. biographical.

Though some doubt the truth of the story of Marathon, what is most likely factual?
- A. Pheidippedes ran 140 miles to Sparta to get help.
- B. Persia had twice the soldiers that Athens had.
- C. Athens lost 192 men to Persia's 6400 in a battle.
- D. Athens won a battle against the Persian army.

According to the passage, Herodotus is known for ___ about ____.
- A. writing … Ancient Sparta
- B. accounting … Greek sports
- C. fictionalizing … history
- D. questioning … Athens

Which conclusion can be drawn based on the passage?
- A. Pheidippides was probably not even a real person in history.
- B. The Athenian win over the Persians at Marathon was unexpected.
- C. Most marathon runners compete at the modern-day Olympics.
- D. The Greeks were not expected to win any Olympic events in 1896.

When the Persian army landed in the Greek city-state of Marathon in 490 B.C., the Athenian army was outnumbered two to one. They sent a foot messenger named Pheidippides to Sparta to get help. It is said that the runner covered the distance of about 140 miles roundtrip in only two days.

Meanwhile the battle at Marathon raged and though outnumbered, the Athenians defeated the mighty Persian army. As the story goes, the Athenians lost just 192 men, while the Persians 6.400 were killed! Eager to send word of the victory back to Athens, Pheidippides was called upon again, this time to run the 26 miles home. When he reached the city steps, he called out, "We are victorious!" and then he collapsed and died on the spot.

Much of what we know about Pheidippides and Ancient Greece comes from the Greek historian, Herodotus, though many question his accounts. In this case why wasn't another messenger sent since Pheidippides had just returned from a 140-mile run? Why didn't he ride a horse? Why would the messenger have died when he was a trained runner? These questions and more have cast some doubt about the tale of the marathon man.

Regardless, this story inspired the modern-day marathon. The event was first run in the 1896 Summer Olympics held in (where else?) Athens, Greece, and was won by a Greek athlete. Though he was slowed down by a crowd that mobbed him at the end of the route, he was the only Greek winner in any track and field event at the 1896 games.

The story of Pheidippides would **BEST** be described as

    A. history.
    B. a legend. *

    C. an inspirational tale.
    D. biographical.

(Review the definition for legends, stories passed down for generations.)

Though some doubt the truth of the story of Marathon, what is most likely factual?

    A. Pheidippedes ran 140 miles to Sparta to get help.
    B. Persia had twice the soldiers that Athens had.
    C. Athens lost 192 men to Persia's 6400 in a battle.
    D. Athens won a battle against the Persian army. *

(Since legends are based on facts, we can assume that at least this is true.)

According to the passage, Herodotus is known for ____ about ____.

    A. writing … Ancient Sparta
    B. accounting … Greek sports

    C. fictionalizing … history *
    D. questioning … Athens

(He was a biased historian, playing up the heroics of his people.)

Which conclusion can be drawn based on the passage?

    A. Pheidippides was probably not even a real person in history.
    B. The Athenian win over the Persians at Marathon was unexpected. *
    C. Most marathon runners compete at the modern-day Olympics.
    D. The Greeks were not expected to win any Olympic events in 1896.

(The Athenians were outnumbered and the Persians had a mighty army.).

I, PERICLES

I, Pericles, am ruler of the great and powerful city-state of Athens and now, all of Greece. My story begins at the time when Athens reached its height of power. It did not take long before our neighbors noticed our rise

The nearby Persian Empire, founded by King Cyrus, reached its peak at the same time, by conquering. It expanded so that it stretched from the Indus Valley in India north and west to the Black Sea (see the map below). Then they set their sights on Greece, jealous as they were of our growing power and advanced culture.

First, the vile Persians attacked and seized control of our colonies on the west coast of the Asia Minor. When one of those colonies there revolted against the conquerors, Athens sent its ships to help. Yet even before our fleet could arrive and provide aid, the revolt

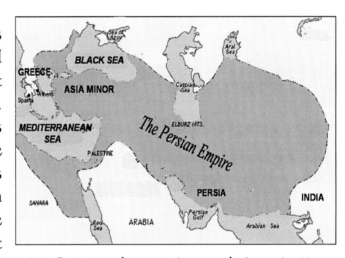

was put down by the Persian ruler Darius. Angered over Athens' efforts to interfere, Darius then set out to punish our people by conquering the mainland city-states of Greece

His first attempt went terribly wrong. His entire fleet of ships was destroyed by a horrible storm. Two years later, the Persians had built a new navy and again set sail for our mainland. Their soldiers landed at Marathon, about 26 miles from Athens. There the Athenians, though greatly outnumbered, achieved victory over the Persians, killing thousands more than enemy soldiers than the Greeks lost in battle. This defeat embarrassed Darius, but did not deter him. He remained more determined than ever to punish and conquer the Greek mainland.

When Darius died, his son Xerxes continued his plans, launching yet another attack, this time by land. Taking no chances, this time the Persians sent 250,000 soldiers. In but a few weeks they were able to gain control of northern Greece and were poised to move south to Athens.

The city-state's leader at the time, Themistocles, believed that if the Athenians could lure the Persians from the land to fight a sea battle; they would have their best chance to win. But time was short and they needed it to assemble their fleet and prepare for battle. So the Athenians evacuated their city, leaving it for the Persians to burn to the ground.

The Spartans, allies of Athens, helped by providing the opportunity for the Athenians to escape. They waged a land battle at Thermopylae, a narrow mountain pass north of Athens. Terribly outnumbered, the brave Spartans managed to hold off the attackers for almost three days so the Athenian armies could get to sea. Legend has it, though, that a Spartan traitor showed the Persians a secret trail around the pass. This allowed the Spartans to stage a surprise attack from the rear. All 300 Spartan soldiers were killed in the slaughter.

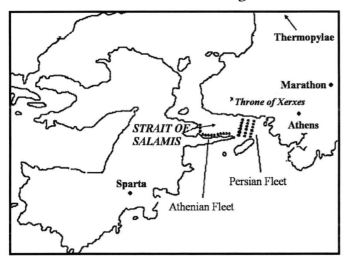

Meanwhile, the Persian fleet went after the Greeks. They had positioned their ships in the narrow Strait of Salamis. Xerxes, certain his fleet would win an easy victory, had a golden throne built on the cliffs above to watch his navy's rout. But Xerxes was wrong. Instead the Greek ships wiped out the Persian fleet and then defeated what remained of their armies, ending the Persian threat to our land. It was remarkable that our forces defeated such a powerful foe!

By ending this threat, our people have been able to progress without fear of attack. I am most proud to be leading my people in such an exciting time. We are in a period of rapid economic development. Our power now extends around the Mediterranean Sea and across the whole Aegean region as well. Athens now leads all Greeks through our leadership in the Delian League, our great alliance of city-states. Formed during the war, it now serves to hold us all together under Athens' peaceful rule. Our scholars oft say we are at the peak of all civilization, poised to leave our mark upon the breadth of human history. I should not be surprised if long in the future people look upon our many achievements and say, "There was no more glorious time in history than the Golden Age of Greece."

MAKING A LONG STORY SHORT

THE PERSIAN WARS

I. THE PARTICIPANTS
    A. _____
    B. _____

II. THE CAUSES
    A. _____
    B. _____

III. THE BATTLES
    A. _____
        1. Detail - _____

            _____

        2. Outcome - _____

            _____

    B. _____
        1. Detail - _____

            _____

        2. Outcome - _____

            _____

    C. _____
        1. Detail - _____

            _____

        2. Outcome - _____

            _____

IV. SIGNIFICANCE
    A. _____
    B. _____
    C. Golden Age of Greece
        1. _____
        2. _____

MAKING A LONG STORY SHORT
SUGGESTIONS FOR ANSWERS

THE PERSIAN WARS

I. THE PARTICIPANTS
   A. *The Persian Empire, led by Darius and his son Xerxes*
   B. *The Greeks, especially Athens and Sparta*

II. THE CAUSES
   A. *The Persians were jealous of Greek power, attacked and conquered Greek colonies in Ionia*
   B. *Athens sent help to Ionia, Persians vowed revenge*

III. THE BATTLES
   A. *Persian fleet heads for Greece*
      1. **Detail -**
      2. **Outcome** *- Storm wiped out the fleet*
   B. *Persians attack Greece at Marathon*
      1. **Detail -**
      2. **Outcome** *- Although outnumbered, Greece wins the battle*
   C. *Persians attack at Straits of Salamis*
      1. **Detail -**
      2. **Outcome:** *Spartans hold off Persians so the Greeks can get ready and then destroy the Persian fleet*

IV. SIGNIFICANCE
   A. *Permanently ended the threat of the Persians in Greece*
   B. *Greeks controlled Mediterranean plus Aegean region*
   C. Golden Age of Greece
      1. *Time of peace and great achievements*
      2. *Peak of civilization; would influence many, many generations to come!*

Telling Tales

Springboard:
Students should complete the "Tall Tales" handout.
*(Story One is a parable; Two is a legend; Three is a myth;
and Story Four is a fable.)*

Objective: The student will be able to identify several types of Greek literature.

Materials:
Tall Tales (Springboard handout)
The Moral of the Story (handout)
Greek Lit 101 (handout)

Terms to know:
anthropomorphic - non-human things such as animals that are given human characteristics
moral - lesson or standard for good behavior

Procedure:

- After reviewing the Springboard, explain that *in this lesson the student(s) will examine fables and other genres of Greek literature.*
- Distribute "The Moral of the Story" and explain that *these stories were written by a Greek storyteller and slave named Aesop. His collections of fables are still taught as lessons and appear in various forms in modern literature, films, and cartoons.*
- Student(s) should work independently or in pairs to read each fable to figure out a moral for each story.
- Have the student(s) share and compare their ideas. *(Some possible answers are: 1) Don't wait until the last minute to prepare. 2) If you're too greedy, you might lose what you already have. 3) Beauty without brains won't get you very far. 4) Be carefully who you hang out with; you might be guilty by association.)*
- Distribute "Greek Lit 101." Have the student(s) read the handout together or independently.
- Then lead a discussion, including the following questions:
  - ? What do most forms of Greek literature have in common? *(Answers will vary, but most was used to teach Greek values and morals.)*
  - ? How did Ancient Greek literature change and evolve? *(Answers may vary, but should reflect the fact that it became more sophisticated and complex. It began as the simple re-telling of war stories by Homer, progressed to lyrical poetry of Sapphro, and then to the more satirical commentary on society by Aristophanes.)*
  - ? Based on the examples of Greek literature, what do you think the Greeks valued? (Answers could include: bravery, heroism, patriotism, athleticism, intelligence, creative thinking, courage, facing one's fate, passion, love, revenge, etc.)*

TALL tales

DIRECTIONS: Read each definition and match each to the examples below.

Fable:	a short story that usually includes anthropomorphic animals and teaches a moral lesson
Parable:	a short story that has a moral lesson, but usually does not include anthropomorphic animals
Myth:	a story about gods, goddesses, and heroes that explains natural events or human behavior
Legend:	an old story, passed down as history, but is mostly fiction

Story One: _____ On final exam day a professor told her class, "It's been a pleasure teaching you. I know you have all worked very hard and many of you are worried about your grade point average dropping. Therefore, anyone who would like to opt out of this test will receive a "B" for the course." Immediately, all but two students leapt up, thanked the professor, and rushed from the room. She then closed the door behind them, turned to the two remaining students, and said "I'm glad to see you believe in yourselves. You both have A's."

Story Two: _____ Many years ago an ordinary man named Robin lived in Sherwood Forest. He did not like the way the rich treated the poor Saxon people who worked hard every day. They lived in small huts while the Normans wasted money on huge castles and feasts. When Robin was declared an outlaw by the nasty Prince John, he lost everything he owned and was banished to the forest. The Saxon people took pity on him and gave him food and shelter. In return, Robin swore to help them. He and his band of outlaws began to steal from the rich and distribute what they took among the poor.

Story Three: _____ Zeus fell in love Metis, but she changed her form many times to avoid him. Finally, though, she agreed to marry him and bear his child. A seer told Zeus that this child would be a girl and cause no problems, but her next child, a boy, would overthrow him. Wanting to take no chances, Zeus swallowed Metis. Later, he got a terrible headache and howled so loud that the other gods came to see what was wrong. To help, they decided to split open Zeus's skull and when they did, out sprang Athena. Considering the circumstances of her birth, Athena became the goddess of intellect and wisdom.

Story Four: _____ One summer day a thirsty Lion and a Boar came up to a well at the same time. They began to argue over who should drink first and soon were locked in a fight till the death. When they stopped suddenly to catch their breath, they saw some Vultures waiting in the distance to feast on whoever lost the fight. They stopped their battle at once, saying, "It is better for us to make friends, than to become the food of Vultures."

The Moral of the Story

The Ant and The Grasshopper

One summer day a cheerful grasshopper was prancing around, singing when he saw an ant struggling with a heavy kernel of corn. "Why not come and play and sing, instead of working so hard?" asked the grasshopper.

"I have to save up enough food for winter time," answered the ant. The grasshopper hopped away thinking that the ant was crazy for worrying about the wintertime now, instead of enjoying summer. A few months later, though, the weather turned cold and winter came. The grasshopper was starving as he could not dig through the frozen ground for food. He made his way to the ant's hill saw the ant was comfortable and fed. He then realized that…

_____

_____

The Dog and the Bone

One day a dog was carrying a bone over a bridge when he saw his reflection in the water. He thought it was another dog with another bone. Wanting the other dog's bone as well, he opened his mouth to bark at it, dropping his bone into the water. As he aw his bone sink to the bottom and away for good, he realized…

_____

_____

The Fox and the Crow

A hungry crow is thrilled to find a piece of cheese on the ground and flies up to a branch in a high tree to enjoy his feast. A sly fox approaches and wants the cheese for himself. He compliments the crow, telling him he is king of the birds. After a few minutes of flattery, the fox asks the crow to sing with his beautiful voice. Feeling full of himself, the crow opens his mouth to sing and drops the cheese. As he watches the fox run off with his cheese, the crow realizes that…

_____

_____

The Farmer and the Stork

A farmer planted traps in his field to catch and kill the crows that were destroying his crops. One day a stork accidentally gets caught in one of the traps. He begs the farmer not to kill him, arguing that he's not a crow. The farmer replied that he didn't care one way or the other and prepared to kill the poor stork. As the stork faces his last moments, he realizes that…

_____

_____

Greek Lit 101

Good day, students. My name is Professor Gleeks and my course is, as you know, is about the Greeks. The ancient Greeks are known for their love of the written word. They left much to read, but the most famous of their old works are the epic poems of Homer. We do not know much about Homer, but we do know he was blind, he was a poet, and he was famous for two epic poems, the *Iliad* and the *Odyssey*.

These works were for a time passed on orally from generation to generation. Both epics offer vivid descriptions of the Trojan Wars. The *Iliad* recounts the adventures of two heroic characters, Achilles and Hector. The *Odyssey* follows the *Iliad,* and tells the story of Odysseus's long journey home after the Trojan Wars. These two works were well-known to all the ancient Greeks. They were used to teach the values and morals of the time to the young people.

At the beginning of the Classical Age (around 500 B.C.) a new form of literature called lyrical poetry emerged. These poems were sung by a performer playing the lyre (an ancient stringed instrument). One of the most famous lyrical poets was Pindar, who wrote about the Olympics. His poems were sung to welcome athletes home from the ancient games. Sapphro, a female poet, was also a famous lyrical poet. Her work was unusual in that she was a woman, and she focused more on personal relationships with friends, family, and rivals instead of Greek culture and values. And oddly for Greeks who tended to ignore women, she was respected and many parents sent their daughters to her to learn to compose poetry of their own.

As the Greeks perfected lyrical poetry, they also invented plays. Early plays were simple songs or had only one character. Playwrights performed their works at feasts to Dionysus, the god of wine, competing against other authors for prizes. As their popularity grew, plays were performed in huge, open-air theaters in front of enormous crowds.

The first plays were dramas, mostly tragic stories about the suffering and downfall of a character. They appealed to many people, because the Greeks believed in facing bad events or terrible fates should be faced with courage and bravery. One of the most famous Greek tragedies is *Medea*, written by the playwright Sophocles. *Medea* is about a woman who was betrayed by her husband and takes revenge by killing his new wife and children -- truly tragic!

Comedies were also very popular. These plays made fun of the people and culture of the time with bold insults, foul language, and brutal honesty. One of the most famous comedians of the time was Aristophanes. He wrote plays making fun of the government, democracy, war, and many other things in Ancient Greece. For example, in his comedy *Lysistrata*, he poked fun at war, by telling about women who refuse to see their husbands until they end their fighting with a neighboring city-state.

It is most unfortunate that much of the literary work of the Greeks is long lost. Still some works of the writers I have told of and others have survived. In fact some are still performed and read by many people even today. And this concludes today's talk. Tomorrow we will begin to read some Greek works.

Deep Thoughts

Springboard:
Students should study "The Sophists" and answer the question.
*(Another word for sophist is "teacher." Answers to the second question
may vary and include: they were very advanced, sought "truth,"
examined the world scientifically, were interested in learning; etc.)*

Objective: The student will be able to explain contributions of Greek philosophy.

Materials: The Sophists (Springboard handout or transparency)
The Trial of Socrates Act I (handout)
The Trial of Socrates Act II (handout)
The Trial of Socrates Act III (handout)
Witnessing the Events (handout)

Terms to know: **Socratic method** - a way of reasoning to find truth by
asking and answering questions.
corruption - moral ruin; dishonesty and bad judgment
philosophy - the study of knowledge and ideas
political science - the study of government and politics
biology - the scientific study of living things

Procedure:
·   While reviewing the Springboard, explain that *the Greeks were the first
people to separate ideas and knowledge from religion and superstition. They
believed that humans could use reason to understand the world around them.
The first and perhaps most famous of these philosophers, or seeker of reason
and knowledge was Socrates. Go on to explain that this lesson, will take a
closer look at the trial and death of Socrates.*

·   Distribute "The Trial of Socrates Part I." **For group instruction** assign parts to
perform or have students read the play in groups. **For individualized
instruction** have the student read the play, or the parent/instructor can read
with the student.

·   Distribute "Witnessing the Events" and have the student(s) complete the
questions for Scene I individually, in pairs or small groups.

·   Have them read "The Trial of Socrates Part II" and complete the questions for
Scene II.

·   Have them read "The Trial of Socrates Part III," study the picture, and
complete the questions for Scene III.

·   Have the student(s) share and compare their ideas from "Witnessing the
Events" and discuss.

48

THE SOPHISTS

Socrates

- Taught his students to know themselves and examine their deepest beliefs.
- Developed the Socratic Method, helping students learn by asking questions that lead them to draw their own conclusions about information.
- Taught his students to questions everything and to think for themselves.
- Sentenced to death in 399 B.C. for teaching "false religion and corrupting the youth of Athens."

Plato

- A student of Socrates, he wrote down everything his teacher said and taught.
- Left Athens for many years after Socrates' death. Eventually came back and opened the "Academy," a school of mathematics and philosophy.
- Wrote one of the first works of political science called "The Republic" in which he argues that society should be governed by the wisest, not the richest or most powerful.

Aristotle

- Was a favorite student of Plato at the Academy.
- Eventually opened his own school called the "Lyceum."
- An excellent example of what the Greeks considered a well-educated man, he studied many different subjects (mathematics, political science, philosophy, medicine, and biology).
- First to classify living things into genus and species.

1. What is another word for "Sophist?" _____

2. **What conclusions can be drawn about Ancient Greece based on these men's works?**

The Trial of Socrates Part I

Characters: Heron (citizen of Athens) and Nicodemus (citizen of Athens)

Setting: Early afternoon at the Athens agora, 399 B.C.

Heron - Where is everyone today, Nicodemus? Why is the marketplace so quiet and empty?

Nicodemus - Could you have forgotten? Today begins the trial for that busybody, Socrates.

Heron - Oh indeed, now I remember. It will seem strange to see him <u>answering</u> questions for a change. Usually, he's here in the marketplace walking around asking everyone hundreds of annoying questions when they're trying to do business. It will be satisfying to see the judges asking the questions and he having to come up with the answers. Perhaps that will end his ceaseless queries!

Nicodemus - I know what you mean. I was talking with Adonis the other day about how wonderful our democracy in Athens is, and out of nowhere the old man shows up. He almost frightened us to death because you can never hear him coming! He doesn't wear sandals you know because (*rolling his eyes*) he prefers to have his bare feet touch the earth. He thinks that the closer you are to the earth, the closer you are to truth. What does he mean by that anyway?!

Heron - I couldn't tell you. So, what were you saying about speaking with Adonis?

Nicodemus - Right, well, as I was saying, we were talking about our democracy and that pesky Socrates asks us, "What is democracy?"

Heron - How could he not know what democracy is? Every Athenian knows what it is!

Nicodemus - Of course we do, but he kept asking us to explain it. Finally I told him that democracy is when we are all free, equal, and ruled by those whom we elect.

Heron - Did that satisfy him?

Nicodemus - It's obvious that you have never been questioned by Socrates. He never stops asking questions! What is free? Who do you mean by "we"? What is equality? He just went on and on and on until Adonis and I were so confused, we couldn't remember what we had been talking about!

Heron - What did the old loon do then?

Nicodemus - He just smiled and shuffled away. We saw him head towards two other unsuspecting citizens. I tell you, I felt sorry for them!

Heron - You know, he really isn't a bad old guy. He's obviously quite smart, but those annoying questions! All-in-all they're harmless though, don't you think?

Nicodemus - No, I must disagree with you my friend. Those questions plant thoughts in people's heads, thoughts that could grow into dangerous, new ideas. The law needs to do something about the way he harasses the good people of Athens. I think it is about time they've dealt with him. Would you like to go and watch the trial?

Heron - Yes, I would. I came into town to see about buying a new slave, but this ought to be much more entertaining, although I still think he truly is a harmless old man.

The Trial of Socrates Part II

Characters: Judge 1
                  Socrates
                  Judge 2
                  Plato (Socrates' student)
                  Apollodorus (Socrates' student)
                  Xanthippe (Socrates' wife)

Setting: That afternoon in the Council Hall of Athens. All are seated, courtroom style.

Judge 1 - Socrates, come here. (Socrates approaches the judge.) You are on trial today for the crime of corrupting the youth of Athens. How do you answer this charge?

Socrates - I am hurt. My entire life has been spent seeking truth and wisdom. I care most deeply about my students and about my city. I could no more seek to corrupt them than I could plunder the Parthenon. The only thing I want for our youth is that they find truth!

Judge 2 - That may be so, but what you have done is encourage them to question the council, the leaders, and the democracy of Athens itself! These young people follow you, listening to your questions; they want to be like you! What will happen when they are grown? We depend upon them to lead and participate in the democracy in the future. What will happen if they lack respect for it due to your constant questioning of it?

Socrates - I do not wish to make them disloyal to Athens. I am simply ask questions to make my students think and make ideas clear to them. How can this corrupt them?

Judge 1 - I'm warning you old man! Do not start questioning us! *(Noise from the back of the room breaks out as Plato and Apollodorus run up to the judges)* Who are these young men?!

Plato - I am Plato and this is Apollodorus. We are two of Socrates' most devoted students.

Judge 1 - Well what do you want? We are in the midst of a trial here.

Apollodorus - We've come to speak on behalf of our beloved teacher. We can help you understand what he does and see for yourselves that he is not corrupting anyone!

Judge 2 - All right then. Speak.

Apollodorus - Thank you your honor. Socrates is a wonderful man who would never do any wrong to anyone! Yes, he teaches us to question, but only so we can learn the truth. He makes us think about ourselves and our world by having us, "What is justice? What is truth? What is courage?"

Judge 1 - Has he ever encouraged you to question our democracy?

Plato - He encourages us to come to our own conclusions. He never pushes his views upon us. *(A woman enters.)* Xanthippe! What are you doing here? We told you we would plead his case.

Xanthippe - Judges, please forgive me, but I have come to plead for my husband's life! I know he can be troublesome, but he is a good man and an honorable citizen. Please, I beg of you to let him go. He is an old man. I will take him home and keep him out of trouble for the few years he has left... *(Socrates interrupts)*

Socrates - I am tired and I have heard enough. Either let me go or condemn me, but I will not change my ways, so hurry up and make up your mind. *(The crowd stirs.)*

Judge 1 - Enough! We've heard enough. The council must now vote.

The Trial of Socrates Part III

Characters: Plato   Socrates
Crito (friend of Socrates)   Guard

Setting: Three weeks later, in a small prison cell.

Plato - Socrates, my dear Socrates, how can you be so calm? Every day your students come to see you, expecting you to speak of your death. Yet you continue asking questions of us as always; you continue on as if nothing has happened and nothing dire is going to happen.

Socrates - Why should I be anything but calm? I am not afraid to die. I'd much prefer to die now while I still have my mind and can still think and teach, than die an old man who's lost his head and cannot do those things! *(Crito rushes in)*

Crito - Socrates, I have wonderful news! I have bribed the guards! I am here to save you. Come with me now; you can escape, but we must hurry!

Plato - Wonderful Crito! Hurry now Socrates, it is our last hope to save you!

Socrates - Wait! Wait, my young friends. Let us take a moment to think about this. In what way would my escape further the truth?

Crito - Socrates, there is no time for this! We can discuss truth later. Come, we must leave this place right now!

Socrates - Have you two forgotten all that I have taught you? We should always act on reason, not impulse. If I were to run away now, it would be an act of impulse, not a thoughtful one. I cannot run away. My life is and always has been here in Athens, and my purpose was and remains to pursue truth and wisdom. Everyone thinks I am just an old man, a crazy nuisance. And yes, I know that I am a bother, and my questions annoy some. But I have stirred Athens to action when she became too settled in her thoughts, too sure that she was always in the right. Those who judge me think I do not care for this city, but the truth is that I love Athens and could not live without her. *(A guard enters carrying a goblet of hemlock, a poison.)*

Guard - Here, Socrates, drink this. (hands the cup to Socrates) It is hemlock; the poison does not take long to do its work.

Socrates - As I drink this hemlock, my thirst will be quenched forever. *(Socrates drinks from the goblet, sits quietly for a few moments, and then dies.*

"The Death of Socrates"
a painting by
Jacques Louis David

Witnessing the Events

SCENE I QUESTIONS:

? Explain, in your own words, what Socrates is accused of.

? Why do you think some Athenians would have considered Socrates a "pest"?

? Which man's view of Socrates do you most agree with: Nicodemus or Heron? Why?

SCENE II QUESTIONS:

? Why do you think Socrates is hurt by the charges against him?

? What points are Plato and Apollodorus trying to make about Socrates?

? If you were a judge, how would you vote in this trial? Why?

SCENE III QUESTIONS:

? Explain why Socrates isn't afraid to die.

? Why isn't Socrates concerned about being seen as a pest?

? Look at the painting, the *Death of Socrates*, and create a caption for it. What do you think Socrates is saying in this scene?

Olympus

Springboard:
Students should read "Dionysus" and answer the question.
(Dionysus was important because he introduced wine to the Greeks. Wine was a staple of Greece's trade and economy. Dionysus also illustrated the dual nature of wine and other alcohol: it could bring joy and be part of celebrations, but it could also bring despair and anger.)

Objective: The student will be able to explain the importance of mythology in Ancient Greece and relate one or more Greek myths.

Materials: Dionysus (Springboard handout)
                Select-a-Story (handout or transparency)

Terms to know: mortal - human

Procedure:

· During discussion of the Springboard, explain that *the Greeks used myths to explain many elements of their life, history and culture*. Go on to explain that *in this lesson, the student(s) will read more Greek stories to learn about Zeus, Hera, and other Greek gods, goddesses, and heroes*.

· Display the "Select-a-Story" transparency. The student(s) should work individually or in small groups to choose one of the subjects on the transparency to research.

· Students should then use the Internet or media resources to find a myth about their topic and prepare a skit to perform for the class. **For individualized instruction** the student should prepare a monologue for one of the characters involved to tell the story. (**NOTE:** This portion of the activity can take one or more class periods, depending upon available time and student interest. You may want to provide art materials for scenery and props. There are numerous websites devoted to the topic but this one has everything: **www.mythweb.com/encyc/**.

· The student(s) should perform their skits or monologue.

· Then lead a discussion of the importance of mythology to the Ancient Greeks, using the lesson objective question as a guide. (*Mythology was the basis of the religion of the Ancient Greeks. It explained natural phenomena as well as some aspects of Greek culture.*)

DIONYSUS

DIRECTIONS: Read the information about the Greek god, Dionysus, and explain why he was so important to the people of Ancient Greece below.

According to Greek mythology, Dionysus was the son of Zeus and a mortal woman named Semele. Hera, Zeus's wife, was enraged when she discovered her that her husband had a child by another woman and plotted to kill the both Semele and her baby. She soon visited Semele in disguise and convinced her that Zeus was not the father of the child.

Feeling betrayed, Semele demanded that Zeus grant her one wish of her choice. Zeus, who at the time was madly in love with her, agreed, so Semele told him her wish: that he show his true form to her.

Zeus was devastated by this because mortals could not survive seeing the true form of the gods. However, he had sworn to grant her the wish, so he appeared in front of Semele, and she instantly burned up so there was nothing left of her. Zeus was able to rescue the baby and sewed it into his thigh to keep it safe. And then a few months later the infant named Dionysus was born again.

However, Hera was still angry and wanted to kill Dionysus so she ordered the Titans (the elder gods) to do the deed. The Titans ripped Dionysus to pieces, but he was rescued and brought back to life by Rhea, the mother of Zeus. After this close call, Zeus realized that Dionysus had to be hidden away to escape Hera's wrath. He arranged for the wood nymphs to take Dionysus and raise him in the woods.

While with the nymphs, Dionysus discovered how to extract juice from the vines of grapes. When he was grown, he wandered the earth, spreading his knowledge of winemaking to places near and far from Greece. One of the most important Greek gods, Dionysus has a dual nature. He can on one hand bring joy and delight, but he can also drive people to intense and uncontrollable anger and despair.

_____

_____

_____

_____

_____

_____

_____

_____

_____

Select-a-Story

Achilles
Aphrodite
Apollo
Ares
Argus
Artemis
Athena
Atlantis
Centaurs
Circe
Daedalus
Eros
Europa
Golden Fleece
Hades
Helen of Troy
Hephaestus
Hera
Heracles
Hermes
Icarus
Jason
Labrynth
Marathon
Medusa
Midas
Minotaur
Odysseus
Orpheus
Persephone
Perseus
Poseidon
Prometheus
Sirens
Titans
Zeus

Fun and Games

Objective: The student will be able to explain the important elements of the ancient Greek games, and compare and contrast them to the modern Olympics.

Materials: What is This? (Springboard handout)
                       The Ancient Greek Olympics (2-page handout)
                       Comparing Competitions (handout)
                       highlighters

Terms to know: **oracle** - a person believed to have psychic powers
                       pentathlon - a competition of five track and field events: sprint, hurdles, long jump, discus, and javelin
                       truce - agreement to stop fighting

Procedure:

· After reviewing the Springboard, explain *that in this lesson, the student(s) will read about the ancient Greek Olympics and then compare and contrast them to the modern Olympics.*

· Distribute "the Ancient Greek Olympics" and have student(s) read the handout independently, in pairs or small groups. Encourage student(s) to highlight meaningful passages and characteristics of the ancient games.

· Distribute "Comparing Competitions" and have the student(s) complete the Venn diagram. You may wish to complete the handout together if your student(s) do not know much about the modern games.

· Have the student(s) share and compare their answers.

WHAT IS THIS?

DIRECTIONS: Study the photograph to answer the questions below.

What is happening in this picture?

What clues helped you figure out what it is?

Why do you think the authors included the picture in a unit about Ancient Greece?

The Ancient Greek Olympics

There are many, differing accounts of the origin of the Greek Olympics. One such story tells the tale of Pelops, a prince from Asia Minor (now Turkey) who sought the hand of Hippodamia, the daughter of the King of Pisa. An oracle had once told the Pisa king that he would be killed by his son-in-law, so he devised a plan to do away with this suitor as he had ridded his daughter and himself of twelve others already.

An excellent charioteer, the king invited Prince Pelops to compete in a chariot race. He promised that if the young man won the race, he could marry his daughter, Hippodamia. If, on the other hand he lost, Pelops would be beheaded. Now the prince already knew about the other twelve suitors and knew the king felt very sure of himself. Still, the prince conceived a way of winning by secretly replacing the bronze linchpins holding the wheels on the king's chariot with pins of wax.

So during the race when the king was trying to pass Pelops, the wax pins melted, causing the wheels to fall off and the king's death. Pelops then married Hippodamia and organized the first Olympics to celebrate his victory and to honor the memory of his father-in-law.

Whatever the reason, the ancient Olympics are thought to have begun as early as 1200 B.C., but records were not kept until 776 B.C. From these records, modern day historians have learned much about the ancient games. They were held every four years in the city-state of Olympia. At first they only lasted two days, mainly because there was only one event, the foot race. Over time, though, many events were added such as boxing, discus throwing, horseback riding, chariot racing, wrestling, and the pentathlon. Athletes traveled from as far away as southern Spain and the east coast of the Black Sea, as well as from all the Greek city-states to showcase their talents. People also came from all over to watch the games, filling the stands with tens of thousands of cheering fans.

The Olympics were actually religious in nature, held to honor Zeus, king of the Greek gods, and other gods. In fact they were more like a religious festival. Ceremonies were held and sacrifices were made to honor the gods. The Greeks believed athletes received their talents from the gods, so they prayed for victory and thanked them for their successes.

Ancient Olympic athletes lived according to very strict schedules. In addition to the tough physical training, their diets were also restricted to water, cheese, milk, and sometimes fish and meat. Women were not allowed to participate in, or even attend the games, although there was one exception.

A father training his son, a runner named Pisidorus, for one of the early games died suddenly. The young man's mother, not wanting her son to miss his chance to compete in the upcoming games, stepped in to help with training. After months of hard work, the day of the race arrived. After all she had done to prepare him, his mother wanted to see her son compete so badly that she disguised herself as a man and went to the stadium. When he won the race, the mother screamed, cheered, and jumped up and down in excitement. As she did, the hood covering her long hair fell backward and exposed her to all the men around her. She was seized and brought before the Olympic judges. Although the penalty for her actions should have been death, the judges pardoned her when they learned she had trained an Olympic champion.

The rule regarding female participation was only one of many. Athletes and their home cities had to pay hefty fines if they were caught bribing fellow athletes or judges, breaking training rules, or showing any fear (such as backing out of an event). The athletes were required to arrive in Olympia a month before the games began; failure to abide by this deadline resulted in a fee. The most important rule was the "sacred truce." All cities involved agreed to stop any wars being fought at the time to allow athletes and spectators to travel to and from the games in safety. Fees for these and other offenses were usually paid in the form of golden statues to honor Zeus. These were left in Olympia after the games.

The winners of each event at the games received nothing more than wreaths of olive branches. Some cities, however, honored their Olympic heroes with statues in their honor or by paying poets to write verses about them. A simple wreath and the honor of victory was enough for athletes at first, but as Greek society began to erode, they began to demand bigger rewards and became more interested in money, not honor. Eventually, bribery became common and by the end, the ancient games became more like a circus than a festival, losing their religious and sacred atmosphere.

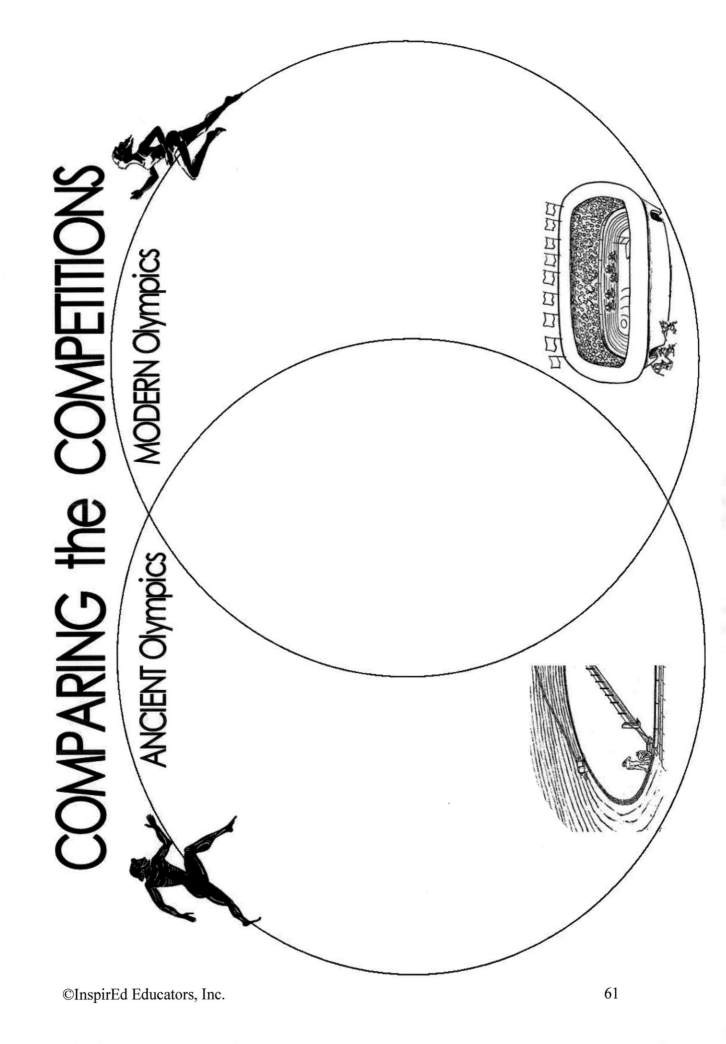

COMPARING the COMPETITIONS

MODERN Olympics

ANCIENT Olympics

COMPARING the COMPETITIONS
Suggestions for Answers

ANCIENT Olympics

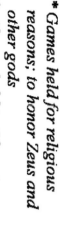

* Games held for religious reasons; to honor Zeus and other gods
* Always held in Olympia
* Lasted for two days
* Only included a few events
* Women were excluded from competition and viewing
* Penalties for breaking rules were fines or statues of Zeus
* Winners received olive-branch wreaths
* Sacred truce ensured peace and safe travel for the games

* Held every four years
* Both involved athletic competitions
* Both held in special facilities
* New events added over time
* Large numbers of people travel from distant places to participate or view
* Athletes follow strict training schedules and diets
* Athletes hailed as heroes

MODERN Olympics

* No religious significance involved
* Location of games changes
* Last for two weeks
* Hold many events
* Women and men compete
* Penalty for breaking rules is disqualification
* Winners earn 1st, 2nd, and 3rd place ribbons and trophies
* Games held in summer and winter
* Have opening and closing ceremonies

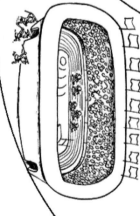

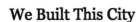

We Built This City

Springboard:
  Students should read "The Parthenon" and answer the questions.

Objective: The student will describe and recognize the three orders of Greek architecture.

Materials:
  The Parthenon (Springboard handout)
  Ancient Greek Architecture (handout)
  Placing Places (handout or transparency)

Terms to know: **architecture** - the style and features of buildings

Procedure:

• After reviewing the Springboard, explain that _in this lesson the student(s) will learn about different styles of Ancient Greek architecture._

• Distribute "Ancient Greek Architecture" and "Placing Places." The student(s) should work independently, in pairs, or small groups to study the architectural information and the pictures of the modern buildings decide which Greek architectural style is reflected in each building.

• Have the student(s) share and compare their ideas. The student(s) should use specific features from "Ancient Greek Architecture" to justify their choices. (_Answers (l. to r. from top): Corinthian, Doric, Ionic, Corinthian, Doric, Ionic_) During the discussion, have the student(s) identify any other features they see in common among the buildings with the same architectural style. (_For example, the tops of the Ionic and Corinthian buildings are more decorative and have cut-out trim work. Doric buildings are much plainer overall._)

• **EXTENSION or HOMEWORK:** Have the student(s) find other pictures buildings from ancient Greece or other buildings in Greek style. **For group instruction** have them show their pictures as others guess. **For individual instruction** have the student tell the style of each and explain his/her reasoning.

The Parthenon

The Greeks worshipped many gods and goddesses whom they believed controlled their fate. Therefore, they spent a lot of time and energy trying to please their deities. One way they showed their **reverence** was by building beautiful temples for them. One of the most famous of these is the Parthenon, located in Athens.

Athena, the goddess of wisdom, war, and art was the patron goddess of Athens, and the Parthenon was built to honor her. Remains of the white marble temple still can be seen today. Work on the building began in 447 B.C. and was not complete until 437 B.C. The city spared no expense on the temple.

Built on the acropolis, or the sacred hill of the city, the Parthenon is a large rectangular structure. The temple is enclosed by 46 columns, each one 34 feet tall. The inner area is called the *cella* and contains two rooms. These two rooms are surrounded by a thick stone wall except for at the front and the back, where two openings were left to enter and leaver the building. Each entrance has six more columns outside of it.

The Main Room was also bordered with 21 more columns. This room housed the chamber with a 12 foot golden statue of Athena in it. The smaller of the two interior rooms, the Treasury, was where money and other belongings of the city were stored.

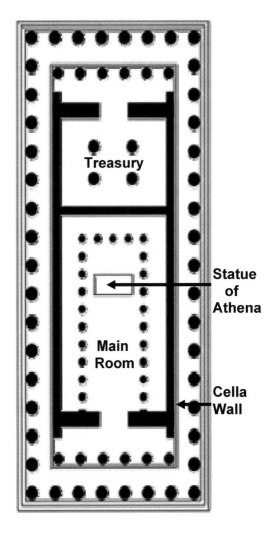

Based on information from the passage, a synonym for the word *reverence* could be
- A. respect.
- B. disgust.
- C. hatred.
- D. dislike.

The circular symbols on the floor plan of the Parthenon represent
- A. walls.
- B. cellas.
- C. columns.
- D. platforms.

Explain how three characteristics of the Parthenon show Athena's importance to the city.

The Parthenon - Answers & Explanations

The Greeks worshipped many gods and goddesses whom they believed controlled their fate. Therefore, they spent a lot of time and energy trying to please their deities. One way they showed their **reverence** was by building beautiful temples for them. One of the most famous of these is the Parthenon, located in Athens.

Athena, the goddess of wisdom, war, and art was the patron goddess of Athens, and the Parthenon was built to honor her. Remains of the white marble temple still can be seen today. Work on the building began in 447 B.C. and was not complete until 437 B.C. The city spared no expense on the temple.

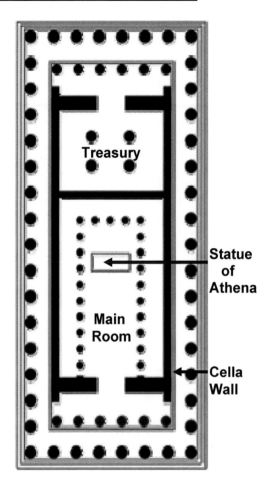

Built on the acropolis, or the sacred hill of the city, the Parthenon is a large rectangular structure. The temple is enclosed by 46 columns, each one 34 feet tall. The inner area is called the *cella* and contains two rooms. These two rooms are surrounded by a thick stone wall except for at the front and the back, where two openings were left to enter and leaver the building. Each entrance has six more columns outside of it.

The Main Room was also bordered with 21 more columns. This room housed the chamber with a 12 foot golden statue of Athena in it. The smaller of the two interior rooms, the Treasury, was where money and other belongings of the city were stored.

Based on information from the passage, a synonym for the word *reverence* could be

A. respect. *   C. hatred.
B. disgust.   D. dislike.
(***The Greeks showed respect because they believed the gods held their fate in their hands.***)

The circular symbols on the floor plan of the Parthenon represent

A. walls.   C. columns. *
B. cellas.   D. platforms.
 (***The passage describes the location and number of columns there in each section.***)

Explain how three characteristics of the Parthenon show Athena's importance to the city. (***The fact that the Parthenon was built on highest point in the city and no expense was spared illustrates her importance. Also a huge statue of her was built in her honor and placed in the center of the temple.***)

ANCIENT GREEK ARCHITECTURE

The Ancient Greeks developed three main styles, or orders, of architecture. Each style had its own distinct look and details, though columns were common to all. All three orders, although created thousands of years ago, are still frequently included in modern architectural designs.

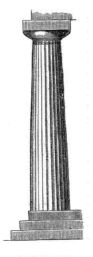

Doric:

The Doric order is the oldest and simplest form of Greek architecture. It is known for its plain-looking columns. Doric columns do not have a base, but sit right on the floor. They are very sturdy and their tops, or capitals, are usually simple squares or circles. These columns are slightly tapered at the top and are thicker overall than the other orders. Each usually has 20 grooves around it called channels that meet at the vertical pillow at the top.

Ionic:

The Ionic order has thinner and more elegant columns than the Doric order. Its capitals are usually decorated with a scroll-like design called a volute. The volute is usually right above an "egg and dart" molding; a series of half ovals and arrowheads. Ionic columns, unlike the earlier Doric style, have a base between the shaft of the column and the floor. Overall, they are more slender than Doric and have more and thinner grooves around the sides; usually about 24.

Corinthian:

The last of the Greek orders to be developed, the Corinthian order, was only rarely used by the ancient Greeks. However, it did become very popular during the later Roman civilization. The shafts of the columns and their bases are similar to Ionic columns; slender and with more grooves than the Dorian. The main identifying feature of Corinthian columns is the very fancy stonework on the capitals. The tops of the columns are generally decorated with flowers, leaves, and vines, which give them a very ornate look.

PLACING PLACES

1. _____

2. _____

3. _____

4. _____

5. _____

6. _____

Wise Guys

> **Springboard:**
> Students will complete "The Hippocratic Oath" handout.
> *(Answers will vary and include: share knowledge with others; ̣espect patient privacy; treat patients as people, not diseases; etc.)*

Objective: The student will be able to explain some Ancient Greek contributions to the world.

Materials:	The Hippocratic Oath (Springboard handout) Founding "Fathers" (2 handouts) Super Greeks (handout)
Terms to know:	**superstition** - irrational belief **ethics** - code of morality and good behavior **theorem** - proposition, formula, that has been proven to be true **physics** - the scientific study of matter, energy, force, and motion

Procedure:

· While reviewing the Springboard, explain that *this oath (or other forms of it) is taken by new doctors. The oath comes from the work of Hippocrates, a Greek physician known as the "Father of Medicine."* Go on to explain that *in this lesson the student(s) will learn about Hippocrates and other famous Greeks who contributed valuable principles and ideas to modern science, mathematics, history, and medicine at the height of that ancient civilization.*

· Distribute copies of the "Founding 'Fathers'" and "Super Greeks" handouts. The student(s) should work individually, in pairs, or small groups to read about the various "Fathers" and complete the assessment of each, adding at one other famous Greek whom they think offered the greatest contributions to the world.

· Have the student(s) share / compare their ideas about the various Greeks' importance and discuss.

The Hippocratic Oath

I swear to fulfill, to the best of my ability and judgment, this covenant:

- I will respect the hard-won scientific gains of those physicians in whose steps I walk, and gladly share such knowledge as is mine with those who are to follow.

- I will remember that there is art to medicine as well as science; and that warmth, sympathy, and understanding may outweigh the surgeon's knife or the chemist's drug.

- I will not be ashamed to say "I know not," nor will I fail to call in my colleagues when the skills of another are needed for a patient's recovery.

- I will respect the privacy of my patients, for their problems are not disclosed to me that the world may know. Most especially must I tread with care in matters of life and death. If it is given me to save a life, all thanks. But it may also be within my power to take a life; this awesome responsibility must be faced with great humbleness and awareness of my own frailty. Above all, I must not play at God.

- I will remember that I do not treat a fever chart, a cancerous growth, but a sick human being, whose illness may affect the person's family and economic stability. My responsibility includes these related problems, if I am to care adequately for the sick.

- I will prevent disease whenever I can, for prevention is preferable to cure.

- I will remember that I remain a member of society, with special obligations to all my fellow human beings, those sound of mind and body as well as the infirm.

- If I do not violate this oath, may I enjoy life and art, respected while I live and remembered with affection thereafter. May I always act so as to preserve the finest traditions of my calling and may I long experience the joy of healing those who seek my help.

  - The modern version of the doctors' oath was written in 1964 by Louis Lasagna, Tufts University.

In your own words, list three promises from the Hippocratic Oath:

_____

_____

_____

_____

_____

_____

Founding "Fathers"

HIPPOCRATES was born around 460 B.C. on the Greek island of Kos. He studied many subjects in his youth including philosophy, mathematics, and astronomy, but his true passion was healing the sick and discovering the mysteries of the body human.

Before Hippocrates, doctors, like most ancient Greeks, believed sickness was punishment from the gods. Hippocrates separated religion from medicine. In fact he never even mentioned any superstitions or religion in his writings. He argued instead that illness and disease are caused by the environment, diet, and living habits.

Hippocrates and his students described many conditions such as "clubbed fingers," thickening of the flesh under the fingernails, and ranked illnesses as acute (severe), chronic (ongoing), endemic (common) and epidemic (widespread). Later doctors realized that Hippocrates identified symptom of a number of diseases, such as lung cancer and what has come to be known as the Hippocratic Face. A pinched nose, sunken eyes, dry skin, and cold ears are seen in the late stages of deadly diseases. Keenly interested in diseases of the chest, he was the first to perform surgery on the lungs, and his observations helped future doctors to pinpoint the causes and treatment of pneumonia and other lung ailments.

Hippocrates taught and practiced medicine all over Greece and opened a medical school in his childhood home of Kos. Over the years he developed a code of ethics for all doctors. His Hippocratic Oath, which is still used today, sets standards for the treatment of patients and medical knowledge. For these contributions, he is known as the "The Father of Medicine."

HERODOTUS is usually credited with being the first person to record events for future study. Born around 484 B.C. in Asia Minor (modern-day Turkey), he showed an early thirst for knowledge. During his life he traveled all over the ancient world. His travels took him to Babylon, Syria, Egypt and elsewhere in northern Africa, and of course, Greece.

Wherever he went, Herodotus would ask the local people about their religion and customs. Then he organized what he learned into written studies called *historias*, or "inquiries," recording what he was told by eyewitnesses along with his own observations. He used direct quotes, when possible, and noted any information that was second hand.

One of Herodotus' most famous *historias* was about the war between Greece and Persia. This and all his writings were widely read, as their style was meant not only to educate, but also to entertain. Some scholars, in fact, criticize Herodotus as merely a charming storyteller, but most see his work as the earliest history texts. Because of his contributions, he is known as "The Father of History."

Founding "Fathers"

PYTHAGORAS was born around 580 B.C. off the coast of Asia Minor. Having left his city as a young man, he traveled all around the ancient world studying under some of the most brilliant thinkers of the time. It was during his travels that he learned geometry, the branch of mathematics concerned with points, lines, angles, curves, surfaces, and solids.

He was in Egypt at the time the Persians invaded, and he was taken prisoner to Babylon. There he learned even more about arithmetic and other mathematical sciences. When he was able to leave Babylon, he traveled to Croton where he founded a secret society for both men AND WOMEN, which was very unusual for the time. His students studied religion, philosophy, and of course, mathematics.

Although they were interested in many things, Pythagoras and his followers are best known for their contributions to mathematics. Several new ideas are credited to them, the most famous being the Pythagorean Theorem of right trianges. It states that the square of the hypotenuse (the longest side) is equal to the sum of the squares of the other two sides. This is most useful when calculating angles and especially distances. For this theorem and other mathematical studies, Pythagoras is known as "The Father of Numbers."

ARCHIMEDES was born in Syracuse, a Greek city-state on the island of Sicily, in 287 B.C. Though interested in many subjects, he is best-known for his contributions in mathematics and science. Little is known of his early life except that his father was an astronomer who may have urged him to go to Egypt to study under the great mathematician Euclid.

Regardless of his training, Archimedes had a wide array of accomplishments such as inventing several war machines for defense, the water screw which allows water and other liquids to be moved and is useful for irrigating farmland, and the earliest known model of an odometer to measure distance traveled.

Probably the most famous story about Archimedes is how he developed the Archimedes Principle that explains why objects float. This he discovered while bathing, since the water level rose when he sat in the tub. He explained that an object placed in a tub filled to the top with water would spill exactly as much water as the volume of the object. The Archimedes Principle is important because it enabled the engineering science of hydraulics to exist. Hydraulics applies the same principle to moving objects. Liquid can be used to push or force machines such as bulldozers, backhoes, shovels, loaders, fork lifts, cranes, and even automobile brakes! Who would have thought that so much invention could come from one little bath! Because of this and other discoveries, Archimedes is known as the "Father of Mathematical Physics."

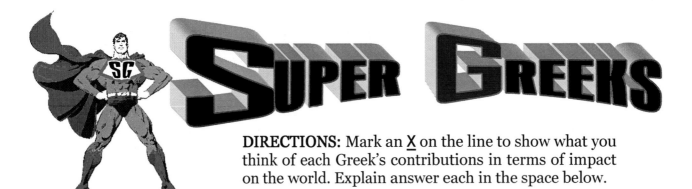

SUPER GREEKS

DIRECTIONS: Mark an <u>X</u> on the line to show what you think of each Greek's contributions in terms of impact on the world. Explain answer each in the space below.

Hippocrates, Father of Medicine:

NOT
Important ⟵————————————————————⟶ **VERY**
Important

Herodotus, Father of History:

NOT
Important ⟵————————————————————⟶ **VERY**
Important

Pythagoras, Father of Numbers:

NOT
Important ⟵————————————————————⟶ **VERY**
Important

Archimedes, Father of Mathematical Physics:
NOT
Important ⟵————————————————————⟶ **VERY**
Important

Greek you consider "super" from another lesson: _____

NOT
Important ⟵————————————————————⟶ **VERY**
Important

Breaking Up

Springboard:
    Students should read "Raising Spartan Soldiers" and answer the questions.

Objective: The student will be able to explain the causes and outcomes of the Peloponnesian Wars.

Materials: Raising Spartan Soldiers (Springboard handout)
                                   War Between the City-States (2-page handout)
                                   Understanding the Story (handout)
                                   Finishing the Story (handout)

Terms to know: **treasury** - store of money
                                   siege - military tactic where troops surround and cut
                                   off access to force a surrender

Procedure:
- While reviewing the Springboard, explain that _in this lesson the student(s) will learn the cause, events, and outcomes of a 27 year war between Athens and Sparta._
- Distribute "War Between the City-States" and Understanding the Story." Have student(s) work independently, in pairs, or small groups to read the diary and journal entries and complete the graphic organizer.
- Have the student(s) share and compare their ideas.
- Distribute "Finishing the Story." Have the student(s) use the information from the lesson to predict what they think happened to ancient Greece after the Peloponnesian War.
- Share and compare answers and discuss.

RAISING SPARTAN SOLDIERS

The soldiers of Sparta were best known for their courage and skill on the battlefield, talents that were nurtured from childhood. Spartan boys went through extremely tough training for military life. Parents had little to say about the matter; since children were seen as belonging to the state, not the parents.

According to custom, fathers brought their newborn infants to a jury to be examined at birth. If the baby seemed healthy, they gave the father orders for how to raise him. If the infant seemed sickly or was disabled in any way, the baby was taken from the parents and exposed, left to die in the wilds.

If the parents were allowed to keep the child, they immediately began preparing the infant for a life of military service. The babies were bathed in wine to toughen their skin. For children discipline was harsh. Children could be severely punished for showing fear of the dark, being picky eaters, or even for just crying. Their hair was shaved and they usually went barefoot and naked.

At the age of seven, most boys left home for military schools. They were taught little in the way of reading and writing. Instead they were taught to endure pain and to fight to win. Their drills, exercises, and lessons were overseen by old men, who would start fights among the children to test their bravery and fighting spirit. The young boys slept in beds they made themselves from plants they collected along river banks. They made tools by breaking sticks and other hard materials with their bare hands.

Each band of young soldiers was led by a captain of about twenty years old. The captain assigned tasks to test the boys' skill and wits. For example they might be ordered to steal food, which posed a dilemma for them. If they were caught stealing, they were beaten and starved. Yet if they didn't attempt the task, they would also starve. Their choice was either to risk a severe beating and starve, or hopefully not starve by getting away with theft. This was all in the name of Spartan "education".

According to the passage, Spartans treated their children like
     A. thieves.   B. adults.   C. property.   D. cowards.

Which statement **BEST** shows the importance of the military in Sparta?
     A. Juries of men examined the physical health and condition of babies.
     B. Education was mostly concerned with physical might and battle skills.
     C. Children were severely punished for harmless and innocent actions.
     D. Old men ran the schools and 20-year-old captains taught the lessons.

Explain how Sparta differs from Athens. _____

_____

_____

_____

_____

The soldiers of Sparta were best known for their courage and skill on the battlefield, talents that were nurtured from childhood. Spartan boys went through extremely tough training for military life. Parents had little to say about the matter; since children were seen as belonging to the state, not the parents.

According to custom, fathers brought their newborn infants to a jury to be examined at birth. If the baby seemed healthy, they gave the father orders for how to raise him. If the infant seemed sickly or was disabled in any way, the baby was taken from the parents and exposed, left to die in the wilds.

If the parents were allowed to keep the child, they immediately began preparing the infant for a life of military service. The babies were bathed in wine to toughen their skin. For children discipline was harsh. Children could be severely punished for showing fear of the dark, being picky eaters, or even for just crying. Their hair was shaved and they usually went barefoot and naked.

At the age of seven, most boys left home for military schools. They were taught little in the way of reading and writing. Instead they were taught to endure pain and to fight to win. Their drills, exercises, and lessons were overseen by old men, who would start fights among the children to test their bravery and fighting spirit. The young boys slept in beds they made themselves from plants they collected along river banks. They made tools by breaking sticks and other hard materials with their bare hands.

Each band of young soldiers was led by a captain of about twenty years old. The captain assigned tasks to test the boys' skill and wits. For example they might be ordered to steal food, which posed a dilemma for them. If they were caught stealing, they were beaten and starved. Yet if they didn't attempt the task, they would also starve. Their choice was either to risk a severe beating and starve, or hopefully not starve by getting away with theft. This was all in the name of Spartan "education".

According to the passage, Spartans treated their children like
    A. thieves   B. adults   C. property *   D. cowards
    (According to the passage, the children were only wards of the parents for a short time, during which they obeyed the state's guidelines.)

Which statement **BEST** shows the imporance of the military in Sparta?
    A. Juries of men examined the physical health and condition of babies.
    B. Education was mostly concerned with physical might and battle skills. *
    C. Children were severely punished for harmless and innocent actions.
    D. Old men ran the schools and 20-year-old captains taught the lessons.
    (The Spartans valued good soldiers above all else, which is why their educational system was set up to mold boys into fearless fighters.)

Explain how Sparta differs from Athens. *Athens emphasized education, love of learning and the arts, and they valued their democracy and individual talents. The culture of Sparta, on the other hand, was geared entirely toward military strength and bravery.*

War Between the City-States

Thoughts of the day...

Relations with Sparta are growing worse by the day. The Spartans resent our control of the Delian League. They fail to understand the importance of the alliance of city-states. Persia remains a danger to us all. We overcame great odds to defeat that evil empire once. We must be prepared to defend ourselves from future attacks.

I am fortunate that the citizens of Athens understand our position. They still look to me to lead them as I have for the past thirty years. Together we have rebuilt our city after it was burned by the Persians. Now Athens is truly breathtaking, with the magnificent Parthenon and other buildings of the Acropolis towering above.

Truly, I think the Spartans are jealous. They claim to be angry at us for moving the Delian League's treasury to Athens. They say they suspect we are growing too greedy and powerful, when I merely seek to keep the League's treasury safe. Athens has the strongest navy in Greece, so it makes sense for us to safeguard the funds here. Indeed, I believe the Spartans envy us!

Yet even in this period of great achievement, they choose to be strong but stupid. No education, no discussions of politics or government! Their children still learn only to be soldiers. To me life without learning, beauty, and culture is not worth living. Hopefully, the tensions will calm soon. I wish I knew what the Spartan leaders are thinking.

Pericles

Dear Diary,

My advisors and I agree that it is time for Sparta to show Athens that it does not hold the sole right to rule Greece. I have met with several other leaders on the Peloponnesian peninsula. We have formed an alliance we are calling the Peloponnesian League, and we will lead it. Already Corinth and Elis have joined, and I expect that the other city-states of the south will soon see the advantage of joining us and our excellent army.

Pericles and his followers claim to be protecting Greece from the Persians, yet Sparta is the strongest and most able city-state. Athens is too powerful now and seeks to be even more so. Why else would they move the Delian treasury there? I even suspect it was Delian League funds that helped that showy city build all of those temples and other buildings!

I hate how the people of Athens look down at us! They all think they are so smart. They forget their victory over the Persians was made possible by our brave Spartan soldiers. I, for one, have had enough of it! It is time to share the power in Greece. One city-state should not have all the money, the greatest numbers of ships in its navy, and all the power. Athens wants to control the whole region and force everyone else to do as they do, read and debate instead of training and exercising! Sparta and our new allies are no longer willing to accept things as they've been.

King Archidamus

Thoughts of the day...

We have now been at war with Sparta for almost two years. Though their army is superior, their navy is no match for ours. Athens is well protected by walls and our navy can easily bring in food from Egypt, despite the siege. The people from the countryside are inside the city walls for protection, so it is very crowded. Still, I think we shall wear the Spartans down. While they hold us under siege outside the walls, our navy is winning victory after victory at sea. It cannot be much longer before they give up and leave, I am sure.

My only true concern is of rumors that the Persians are now helping the Spartans. Word is that they are given them gold to build new ships. If this is true, it is not good news. As I write, the brutes are burning everything in sight outside the city walls, trying to draw us out. As long as we stay here and let our navy fight the war, we are fine. However, if the Persians are helping Sparta match our navy ... I must focus on the moment.

One more point to note: a strange illness is spreading through the city. It must be due to all the crowds. I fear I have begun to fall ill to it, though I am certain it shall pass with haste.

Pericles

Dear Diary,

All is going well for us now in battle. The Athenians are hiding inside their city walls, but they cannot hold out forever. We outnumber them, two to one, and we are burning everything outside of the city so they'll have no food or shelter when they finally come out. Though it is true that their navy is holding us off at sea, that will soon change. The Persians have agreed to help us build ships. Of course our foot soldiers are also doing well, as we would expect. Their training is serving them well, and they are fighting bravely.

I have heard rumor that the mighty Pericles has died. Plague has hit within the city walls and their long—time ruler may be gone. If this is true, it is good news for us. I doubt that they can hold out against our siege when they have fallen so low.

King Archidamus

It is done. Today is terrible day for Athens. After 27 long years of fighting, we have surrendered. We could simply hold out no longer. Over a quarter of our people died from the plague that took our beloved Pericles. After he died, it was hard to go on, but we kept fighting.

Now that all have left the walls of the city, we see what Sparta has done to our fields and orchards. We have nothing to begin anew. We cannot trade. There are no jobs. I know not how we will feed our families?

All here have lost everything, and with no men who can compare to Pericles, we lack a leader. The generals, as the traitor Alcibiades, have either run and joined the Spartans or retired. No one holds any interest in the city any longer, as now all worry only of themselves. What will become of us?

Cleon of Athens

ORGANIZING YOUR THOUGHTS

THE PELOPONNESIAN WARS

Participants - _____

Length of Time - _____

Causes:

Events:

Outcomes:

ORGANIZING YOUR THOUGHTS

THE PELOPONNESIAN WARS

Participants - _____*Sparta and Athens*_____

Length of Time - _____*27 years*_____

Causes:
- *Sparta suspicious and fearful of Delian League*
- *Sparta thinks Athens too greedy and powerful*
- *Athens moves Delian treasury (Sparta thinks they're stealing the money)*
- *Tensions and very different values between Athens and Sparta*
- *Sparta forms own alliance (the Peloponnesian League) which makes Athens suspicious*

Events:
- *People from the countryside flee to Athens for the protection of the city walls; leads to overcrowding*
- *Plague spreads throughout Athens, kills Pericles*
- *Low morale due to loss of Pericles*
- *Persians join the Spartans, help them build ships to fight Athenian navy*
- *Spartan army puts Athens under siege; burns everything else*

Outcomes:
- *25% of Athenians die from the plague*
- *orchards and farmland destroyed*
- *unemployment; no jobs*
- *trade comes to a halt*
- *no strong leadership*
- *Sparta wins the war*

The REST of the Story...

DIRECTIONS: Having examined the Peloponnesian Wars, what do you think happens next? Write two journal entries, one as an Athenian and one as a Spartan, detailing what you predict will be the next chapter in Greek history.

_____

_____

_____

_____

_____

_____

_____

_____

_____

_____

_____

_____

_____

_____

_____

_____

_____

_____

_____

_____

_____

_____

_____

_____

_____

_____

_____

_____

_____

_____

_____

_____

_____

Macedonian Man

Objective: The student will explain the achievements and impact of Alexander the Great and his empire.

Materials: Macedonia (Springboard handout)
                                   Alexander the Great (handout)
                                   In Memoriam (handout)

Terms to know: **province** - area or region of a larger nation or empire
                                   empire - nation that controls itself and others

Procedure:

- After reviewing the Springboard, explain that _the student(s) more closely examine the importance of Alexander the Great in this lesson_.
- Distribute "Alexander the Great" and "In Memoriam." Have the student(s) work individually, in pairs, or small groups to study the content informationand complete the eulogy assignment as directed. Internet and/or media resources should be available for the student(s) to research points as needed.
- Have the student(s) share their speeches and discuss.
- **EXTENSION: For group instruction** a mock funeral could be held for the young, Hellenistic hero. Individual students could each give their eulogies, and pictures, collages, etc. of Alexander the Great, his accomplishments, his empire, and his legacy could be displayed.

Macedonia

Ancient Macedonian Empire

People have lived in Macedonia since prehistoric times, but the people who called themselves Macedonians came to the land in the 7th century B.C. Their kingdom ruled over the region north of Greece until the 4th century, when Philip of Macedonia and his son, Alexander III, conquered many foreign lands and people to establish a vast empire under their control. The Peloponnesian War and Spartan rule thereafter had greatly weakened the Greeks, allowing the Macedonians to defeat them and take control of their land.

Fortunately the Macedonian kings were highly educated and greatly respected the Greeks and of their achievements. So as their empire grew, they spread knowledge and Greek culture to places that came under their control. At its greatest extent, Macedonia ruled lands in Europe, Asia, and Africa. After Alexander the Great's death in 323 B.C., Macedonia's empire split into three parts: Egypt was ruled by the Ptolemy Dynasty; Asia Minor and Persia came under the Seleucid Empire, and Greece was controlled by the Antigonid Dynasty of Macedonia. Then gradually, most of the former Macedonian Empire fell under control of a new and growing power, Rome.

The Macedonian Empire
    A. extended from the Mediterranean to India.
    B. was first established in the 7th century B.C.
    C. ruled over most of Europe, Africa, and Asia.
    D. was ruled by Greek and Roman monarchs.

According to information in the reading, Philip of Macedonia was the
    A. first Macedonian king.
    B. greatest general of the period.
    C. last Macedonian monarch.
    D. father of Alexander the Great.

Based on information in the passage, the Macedonian Empire lasted
    A. less than 100 years.   C. 150 to 200 years.
    B. 100 to 150 years   D. more than 200 years.

Macedonia - Answers & Explanations

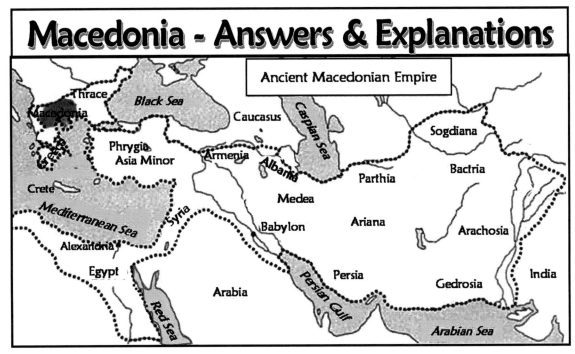

Ancient Macedonian Empire

People have lived in Macedonia since prehistoric times, but the people who called themselves Macedonians came to the land in the 7th century BCE. Their kingdom ruled over the region north of Greece until the 4th century, when Philip of Macedonia and his son, Alexander III, conquered many foreign lands and people to establish a vast empire under their control. The Peloponnesian War and Spartan rule thereafter had greatly weakened the Greeks, allowing the Macedonians to defeat them and take control of their land.

Fortunately the Macedonian kings were highly educated and greatly respected the Greeks and of their achievements. So as their empire grew, they spread knowledge and Greek culture to places that came under their control. At its greatest extent, Macedonia ruled lands in Europe, Asia, and Africa. After Alexander the Great's death in 323 BC, Macedonia's empire split into three parts: Egypt was ruled by the Ptolemy Dynasty; Asia Minor and Persia came under the Seleucid Empire, and Greece was controlled by the Antigonid Dynasty of Macedonia. Then gradually, most of the former Macedonian Empire fell under control of a new and growing power, Rome.

The Macedonian Empire
    A. extended from the Mediterranean to India. *
    B. was first established in the 7th century BCE.
    C. ruled over most of Europe, Africa, and Asia.
    D. was ruled by Greek and Roman monarchs.

(Students have to use the map to answer and must figure out that the dotted line defines the empire.)

According to information in the reading, Philip of Macedonia was the
    A. first Macedonian king.
    B. greatest general of the period.
    C. last Macedonian monarch.
    D. father of Alexander the Great. *

(A and C are false, and B cannot be determined and is also false. Students can conclude that Alexander III was "the Great.")

Based on information in the passage, the Macedonian Empire lasted
    A. less than 100 years. *   C. 150 to 200 years.
    B. 100 to 150 years   D. more than 200 years.
(The empire was established in the 4th century BCE and ended in 323 BCE, still in the 4th century.).

Alexander the Great

359 B.C.   Phillip II becomes king of Macedonia.

338 B.C.   All Greek city-states (except Sparta) united under Macedonian rule.

336 B.C.   Phillip II is assassinated. Alexander (his son) declares himself king.

334 B.C.   Alexander marches into Persia with 40,000 Greek and Macedonian troops, freeing the Greek city-states from Persian rule as he goes.

332 B.C.   Alexander marches into Egypt and frees the Egyptians from Persian rule.

331 B.C.   Alexander marches into Mesopotamia and conquers the Persian cities of Babylon, Susa, and Persepolis.

330 B.C.   Darius (king of Persia) is murdered; Alexander declares himself king of Persia.

327 B.C.   Alexander marches into India, but after 11,000 miles and many battles, his men refuse to go any further.

325 B.C.   Alexander gives into his troops and begins the one-year journey back to Persia.

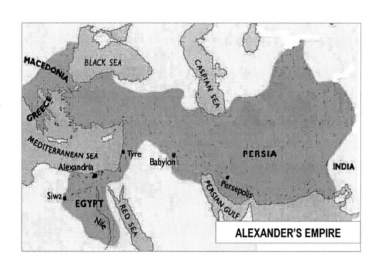

ALEXANDER'S EMPIRE

As Alexander marched through the Persian Empire, he spread Greek culture wherever he went. This time was became known as the Hellenistic Age from the root *"hellas,"* the Greeks' word for their land. As Alexander and his armies marched through the Persian Empire, he encouraged his men to settle along the way and marry the local women. In fact Alexander arranged marriages for thousands of Greek and Macedonian soldiers to Persian women in the city of Susa, and he himself married the daughter of the Persian king, Darius.

As Alexander's empire grew, settlements throughout it were given Greek names, and new cities were built with large libraries to house Greek writings and art. Yet the people were allowed to continue their own forms of local government, so conquered groups were more cooperative. Alexander the Great's dream of uniting the ancient world under his empire, however, was never fulfilled. Alexander died in 323 B.C. at the age of thrity-three with no heir His empire was divided among his top generals soon became three separate kingdoms.

Over time the culture of Alexander's empire changed as it mixed with local cultures and Asian influences. For example the Hellenists focus on the individual was lost to concerns of society and government. The classic Greek love of beauty and simplicity gave way to more realistic sculpture and paintings. People also began to turned away from Greek mythology to practice religions from the Middle East and Asia. Advances in science, medicine, and mathematics continued through the Hellenistic age with new discoveries in physics, astronomy, and engineering.

Though Alexander was never able to complete his dreamed-of empire, in his attempts to do so, he changed a large part of the world. Because of Alexander the Great, the influence of the Ancient Greeks was spread and saved. Had it not have been for him, the cities, the libraries, the rich culture of the Ancient Greek people might have been lost forever.

In Memoriam

DIRECTIONS: Alexanders death came as a blow to his Hellenistic Empire. You have been called upon to write his eulogy speech. Use information from the reading and research as needed using the note taking form below to plan, and then write about him, including AT LEAST:

About him: full name, title, details of birth, life, death, etc:

Summary of accomplishments:

His legacy (what he will be remembered for):

One or more quotes you think sums up his life/purpose:

Anything else?

EXTENSION: Create a collage, drawings, a poster, or other object to celebrate the young Hellenist and his life to be displayed at his funeral

Springboard:
Students should complete "Getting to the Root of It."

Objective: The student will be able to explain ways that Ancient Greeks influence remains today.

Materials: Getting to the Root of It (Springboard handout)
Greek Fair Entry Form (handout)

Procedure:

- After reviewing the Springboard, explain that language is just one of the ways Greek influence is present today. Go on to explain _that in this lesson the student(s) will create a project that illustrates another lasting influence of the ancient Greeks today._
- Distribute the "Greek Fair Entry Form" an review the requirements and specifications for the assignments using the "Grading the Greek Fair" rubric. The student(s) can complete the project individually, in pairs, or small groups, conducting research as needed.
- **For full class instruction** you could have the projects judged by other teachers (or you) so the best project "wins" at the fair.
- Have the student(s) share their work and evaluate the projects using the rubric.

GETTING TO THE ROOT OF IT

DIRECTIONS: All of these word roots come from Ancient Greek. For each study the example and come up with another one of your own.

Root	Meaning	Example	Your Example
anthrop	human	philanthropy	
astro	constellation	astrology	
crat	power, rule	bureaucrat	
chron	time	chronic	
dem	people	democracy	
geo	earth	geography	
mega	big, large	megalopolis	
mono	one	monocle	
morph	form	metamorphosis	
path	feeling, suffering	sympathy	
phil	having s strong love for	philosophy	
phone	voice, sound	phonics	
polis	city	police	
osis	state, condition	neurosis	
therm	heat	thermometer	

GETTING TO THE ROOT OF IT
SUGGESTIONS FOR ANSWERS

Root	Meaning	Example	*Answers may vary.*
anthrop	human	philanthropy	**anthropology, anthropomorphic**
astro	constellation	astrology	**astronomy, astronaut**
crat	power, rule	bureaucrat	**democracy, democrat, autocrat**
chron	time	chronic	**chronicle, synchronize**
dem	people	democracy	**demographic, demogogue, epidemic**
geo	earth	geography	**geology, geophysics, geopolitical**
mega	big, large	megalopolis	**megabyte, megaphone**
mono	one	monocle	**monotone, monologue, monopoly**
morph	form	metamorphosis	**endomorphic, morph**
path	feeling, suffering	sympathy	**pathology, empathy, apathy, psychopath**
phil	having s strong love for	philosophy	**philanthropy, philharmonic**
phone	voice, sound	phonics	**phonograph, phonetic, telephone**
polis	city	police	**metropolis, politics, politician**
osis	state, condition	neurosis	**psychosis, cirrhosis, multiple sclerosis**
therm	heat	thermometer	**thermal, thermostat, geothermal**

GREEK FAIR ENTRY FORM

The Ancient Greeks are known for their long-lasting contributions and achievement in a wide range of subjects from science and medicine to the fine arts. For this assignment you will create a project that shows the influence of this civilization on the world today. Choose one area, pick a format, and complete the entry form at the bottom of the page:

AREAS OF CONTRIBUTION:
- Law
- Government
- Medicine
- Science and Technology
- Architecture
- Philosophy
- Sports and Leisure
- Language
- Art
- Literature

POSSIBLE FORMATS:
- Create and perform a skit
- Draw a picture, or create a sculpture
- Write and perform a rap or song
- Build a diorama
- Or anything else you can think of!

Grading the Greek Fair

Use the following scale to grade your work:

4 - Excellent   3 - Good   2- Fair   1 - Poor   0- Unacceptable

	Student Evaluation	Teacher Evaluation
Followed Assignment	_____	_____
Clearly Depicts Contribution	_____	_____
Shows Research/Preparation	_____	_____
Interesting and Creative	_____	_____
Craftsmanship and Care	_____	_____

GRADE:

COMMENTS:

REVIEWING TERMS

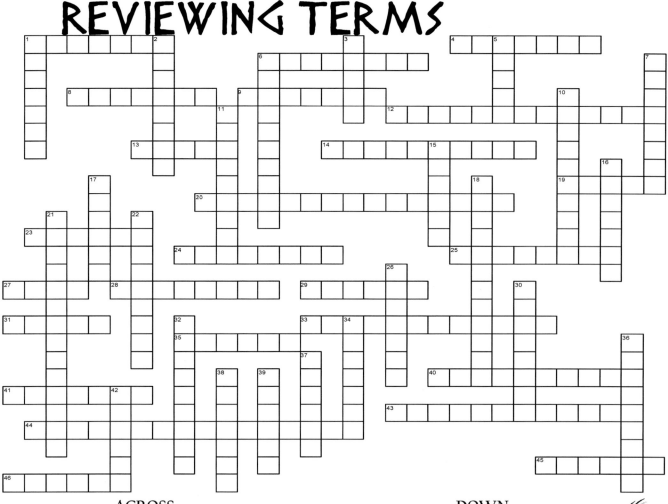

ACROSS

1 formula that has been proven
4 skilled craftsperson
6 area in a larger nation or empire
8 weather over a long period of time
9 study of living things
12 one who studies the past's remains
13 lesson for good behavior
14 self-governing town and the land around it
19 city
20 animals given human characteristics
23 settlement ruled by another country
24 store of money
25 nations working together in a war
27 group of related families
28 upper class, based on birth
29 narrow body of water between two larger ones
31 a god or goddess
33 style and features of buildings
35 nation that controls itself and others
40 five-event track competition
41 selection by random drawing
43 irrational belief
44 study of government and politics
45 one believed to have psychic powers
46 human

DOWN

1 the lay of the land
2 26-mile race
3 military tactic to cut of access
5 agreement to stop fighting
6 study of knowledge and ideas
7 fabrics
10 dishonesty and bad judgment
11 time of peace and achievements
15 foods that are basic to a diet
16 rob and damage
17 change to correct problems
18 society with advanced achievements, including writing
21 way of teaching by asking questions
22 stories about gods, goddesses, and heroes
26 member of state or nation
30 one who buys, sells, or trades
32 government by the people
34 way of life
36 land with water on three sides
37 story based on fact with fictional details
38 study of mattter, energy, and motion
39 code of good behavior
42 religious ceremony

REVIEWING TERMS PUZZLE ANSWERS

Ancient Greece (A)

Matching - Write the letter of the correct answer in the blank:

1. _____ terrain   A. craftsperson

2. _____ oracle   B. narrow body of water

3. _____ ethics   C. agreement to stop fighting

4. _____ artisan   D. store of money

5. _____ merchant   E. surface of the ground

6. _____ textiles   F. code of behavior

7. _____ strait   G. fabric, cloth

8. _____ treasury   H. religious ceremony

9. _____ ritual   I. one who trades for a living

10. _____ truce   J. person believed to have psychic powers

Give an example of each:

11. city-state - _____

12. staple - _____

13. philosopher - _____

14. terrain - _____

15. peninsula - _____

Multiple Choice - Write the letter of the correct answer in the blank:

16. _____ Which of the following is **NOT** an order of Greek architecture?
    A. Doric   B. Ionic   C. Spartan   D. Corinthian

17. _____ Greece's victory in the Persian Wars led to the
    A. Greek Golden Age.   C. Macedonian invasion.
    B. death of Pericles.   D. freedom of the colonies.

18. _____ Hippocrates is known today for
    A. mathematical theorems.   C. the medical oath.
    B. defeating Persia's army.   D. writing about history.

19. _____ Mythology was an important part of Greek life because it gave them
    A. something to pass on to their children.
    B. explanations about nature and culture.
    C. an interesting form of entertainment.
    D. a way to express their literary talent.

Answer the following question:

20. Explain why the Olympics were important to the Ancient Greeks.

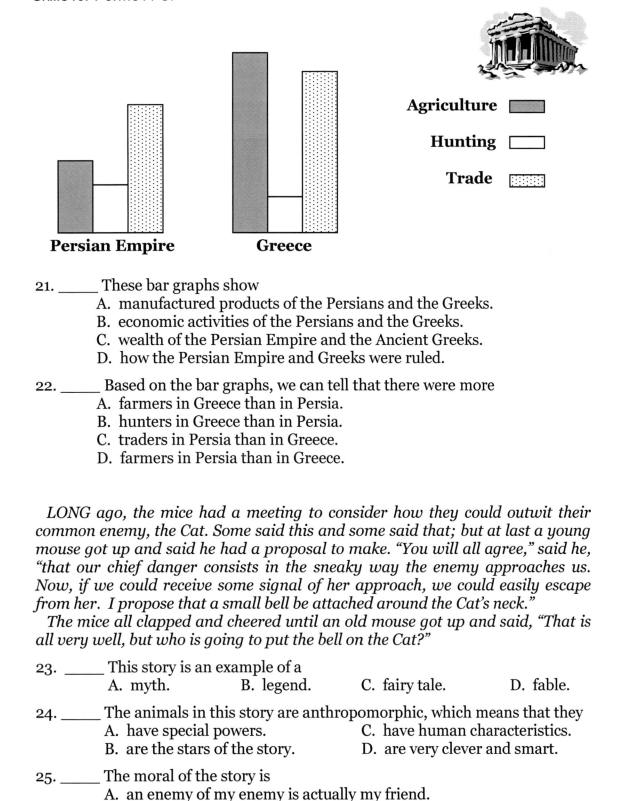

Agriculture ▨

Hunting ☐

Trade ▦

Persian Empire   **Greece**

21. _____ These bar graphs show
    A. manufactured products of the Persians and the Greeks.
    B. economic activities of the Persians and the Greeks.
    C. wealth of the Persian Empire and the Ancient Greeks.
    D. how the Persian Empire and Greeks were ruled.

22. _____ Based on the bar graphs, we can tell that there were more
    A. farmers in Greece than in Persia.
    B. hunters in Greece than in Persia.
    C. traders in Persia than in Greece.
    D. farmers in Persia than in Greece.

LONG ago, the mice had a meeting to consider how they could outwit their common enemy, the Cat. Some said this and some said that; but at last a young mouse got up and said he had a proposal to make. "You will all agree," said he, "that our chief danger consists in the sneaky way the enemy approaches us. Now, if we could receive some signal of her approach, we could easily escape from her. I propose that a small bell be attached around the Cat's neck."

The mice all clapped and cheered until an old mouse got up and said, "That is all very well, but who is going to put the bell on the Cat?"

23. _____ This story is an example of a
    A. myth.   B. legend.   C. fairy tale.   D. fable.

24. _____ The animals in this story are anthropomorphic, which means that they
    A. have special powers.   C. have human characteristics.
    B. are the stars of the story.   D. are very clever and smart.

25. _____ The moral of the story is
    A. an enemy of my enemy is actually my friend.
    B. treat others as you would want to be treated.
    C. solutions are easy if you don't have to implement them.
    D. don't try to outsmart someone who is smarter than you.

Ancient Greece (B)

Fill in the blanks with unit terms:

1. Greece's _____ is very rocky and mountainous.
2. The ancient Greeks often consulted _____ to tell their futures.
3. Philosophers often discussed codes of behavior or _____.
4. Craftspeople, or _____, were imporant to Greece's economy.
5. The _____ sold goods and traded for a living.
6. The _____ flows between the Peloponnesus and mainland of Greece.
7. A/An _____ was called to stop the fighting between two groups.
8. Greek gods and goddesses had _____, or human, characteristics.
9. The first _____ was run by Pheidippides during the Persian Wars.
10. The Delian League's _____, or money, was stored in Athens.

Give an example of each:

11. city-state - _____
12. staple - _____
13. philosopher - _____
14. myth - _____
15. textile - _____

Multiple Choice – Write the letter of the correct answer in the blank:

16. _____ Which of the following was **NOT** a early inhabitant of Greece?

    A. Minoans   B. Spartans   C. Dorians   D. Mycenaeans

17. _____ The Persian Wars were very important in Greek history because the

    A. confidence gained from victory led to Greece's Golden Age.
    B. Persian Empire continued to be a constant threat afterwards.
    C. wars led to the death of their most important leader, Pericles.
    D. Greeks lost their colonies and were not able to trade anymore.

18. _____ Socrates was tried for corrupting the youth of Athens because he encouraged them to

    A. disobey parents and elders.   C. question everything for truth.
    B. participate in democracy.   D. leave home and follow him.

Fully answer the following questions on your own paper and attach:

19. Explain two similarities and two differences between the ancient and modern Olympic games.

20. Explain the factors that let to the decline and fall of the ancient Greeks.

Ancient Greece (C)

Complete the analogies with unit terms:

1. Weather is to daily, as _____ is to over a period of time.
2. A psychic is to today, as the _____ was to Ancient Greece.
3. Art is to painting, sculpture, etc., as _____ is to building.
4. An istmus is to bodies of land, as a/an _____ is to bodies of water.
5. Olives and grapes are to foods, as cotton and wool are to _____.
6. A state is to the U.S., as a/an _____ was to Alexander's empire.
7. The farmer is to growing crops, as the _____ is to selling goods.
8. A piggy bank is to a child, as the _____ was to the Delian League.
9. Four is to an island, as three is to a/an _____.
10. Events are to a historian, as remains are to a/an _____.

Name the category:

11. Athens, Sparta, Elis, Corinth - _____
12. wheat, barley, rice - _____
13. Socrates, Aristotle, Plato - _____
14. stepping on cracks, walking under ladders - _____
15. bribery, embezzlement, voter fraud - _____

Multiple Choice – Write the letter of the correct answer in the blank:

16. _____ Which sentence **BEST** describes the geography of Greece?
    - A. Greece's geography offered both advantages and disadvantages.
    - B. Rugged terrain in and around Greece presented many problems.
    - C. Greece's climate was perfect because of its mild temperatures.
    - D. Its many mountains made moving from place-to-place difficult.
17. _____ The lack of farmable land in Greece eventually led to
    - A. starvation and despair.   C. specialization and trade.
    - B. conquest of neighbors.   D. wealth based on banking.
18. _____ The **MAIN** reason the Ancient Greek Olympics were held was to
    - A. show off athletic skill.   C. showcase the city-states.
    - B. honor their god, Zeus.   D. bring everyone together.

Fully answer the following questions on your own paper and attach:

19. Defend the following statement with specific examples from the unit:
    "The contributions of ancient Greece are still relevant today."

20. Explain the causes of the decline and fall of Greek civilization.

Form A:
1. E
2. J
3. F
4. A
5. I
6. G
7. B
8. D
9. H
10. C

11. Athens, Sparta, Corinth, etc.
12. wheat, rice, barley, etc.
13. Socrates, Plato, Aristotle, etc.
14. mountainous, flat, hilly, etc.
15. Greece, Florida, etc.
16. C
17. A
18. C
19. B
20. They were religious festivals to honor Zeus.

Form B:
1. terrain
2. oracles
3. ethics
4. artisans
5. merchant(s)
6. strait
7. truce
8. mortal
9. marathon
10. treasury

11. Athens, Sparta, Corinth, etc.
12. Athens and Sparta against Persia, etc.
13. Greece, Persia, etc.
14. Dionysus, Athena, Zeus, etc.
15. cotton, silk, satin, etc.
16. B
17. A
18. C
19. They are athletic competitions held every four years and all participate, friends and enemies alike.
20. Defeat in Peloponnesian Wars led to depopulation and unemployment. Pericles' death and Sparta's poor rule made Greece weak and disorganized, so the Macedonians could conquer and take over.

Form C:
1. climate
2. oracle
3. architecture
4. strait
5. textiles
6. province
7. merchant
8. treasury
9. peninsula
10. archaeologist

11. city-state
12. staples
13. philosophers
14. superstitions
15. corruption
16. A
17. C
18. B
19. Greek advances in literature, art, architecture, mathematics, philosophy, etc. are still appreciated, emulated, and built upon today.
20. See Form B answer.

Skills Forms A-C:
21. B
22. A
23. D
24. C
25. C

RESOURCES

www.crystalinks.com/greece.html - "Ancient Greece," Crystalinks, 2008.

www.socyberty.com/History/Ancient-Greece.28390 - "Ancient Greece," Wang, Frank, Stanza Ltd., 2007.

www.ancient-greece.org/history/minoan.html - "History of Minoan Crete." ancient-greece.org, 2008.

www.historywiz.com/myc-civ.htm - "HistoryWiz: The Mycenaean Civilization," historywiz.com, 2005.

www.mnsu.edu/emuseum/prehistory/aegean/theculturesofgreece/dorians.html - " Dorians." Minnesota State University Emuseum, 2008.

www.sikyon.com/index.html - "Ancient Greek Cities." Ellen Papakyriakou/Anagnostou, 1997.

greece.mrdonn.org/city-states.html – "Greek City-States," Mr. Don.org, 2008.

www.pbs.org/empires/thegreeks/htmlver/ - "The Greeks: Crucible of Civilization." pbs.org, 2008.

www.hyperhistory.net/apwh/essays/comp/cw4athensspartap2dz.htm - "Athens and Sparta," Nosotro, Rit, hyperhistory.net, 2008.

en-wikipedia.org/wiki/Ancient_Greece - "Ancient Greece," Wikipedia, the Free Encyclopedia, wikipedia.org, 2005.

www.bbc.co.uk/history/ancient/greeks/greek_olympics_01.shtml - Instone, Dr. Stephen, "The Ancient Greek Olympics," BBC History, BBC, 2004.

www.e-classics.com/pericles.htm - Plutarch, "Pericles: The Olympian," E-Classics, e-classics.com, 2000.

macedonian-heritage.gr/HellenicMacedonia/en/A1.html - "History: Ancient Macedonia," Hellenic Macedonia, Macedonian Heritage, 2005.

wso.williams.edu/~junterek/youth.htm - "Alexander: The Early Years," Alexander the Boy Wonder, Williams College, 2005.

www.infoplease.com/ipa/A0907013.html - "Greek Roots, Prefixes, and Suffixes," Infoplease, Pearson Education, 2008.

i Think: Thematic Units

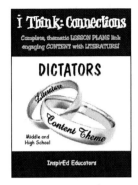  

Some of our other **I Think** offerings include:

Series	Titles
I Think: Connections	Civilization
I Think: Connections	Democracy
I Think: Connections	Dictators
I Think: Connections	Ethnic Conflict
I Think: Connections	Imperialism
I Think: Connections	Indigenous People
I Think: U.S. History	Native Americans
I Think: U.S. History	Colonial America
I Think: U.S. History	American Revolution
I Think: U.S. History	The Civil War
I Think: U.S. History	Reconstruction Era
I Think: U.S. History	Modern America
I Think: Government	Civic Participation
I Think: Government	The Constitution
I Think: Government	The Executive Branch
I Think: Geography	What Is Geography?
I Think: World History	World War I
I Think: Reading & Writing	Poetry

We're adding more titles all the time.
Check our websites for current listings!

www.inspirededucators.com

www.inspiredhomeschoolers.com